Katherine May

Biography

THE HEALING AND SOUL RECOVERING POWER OF WINTERING

TABLE OF CONTENTS

CHAPTER 1
MEMORY OF INDIAN SUMMER

CHAPTER 2
FINDING THE LIGHT BACK

CHAPTER 3
WINTER

CHAPTER 4
HALLOWEEN GHOST STORIES

CHAPTER 5
METAMORPHOSIS

CHAPTER 6
PERFECT SLEEP

CHAPTER 7
MIDWINTER

CHAPTER 8
EPIPHANY

CHAPTER 9
CHALLENGE

CHAPTER 10
IT'S SNOWING

CHAPTER 11
COLD WATER
CHAPTER 13
SURVIVAL
CHAPTER 14
SONG
CHAPTER 15
END

CHAPTER 1
MEMORY OF INDIAN SUMMER

Some winters take place in the sun. This one started on a hot day in early September, a week before my fortieth birthday. I was having a party with friends on Folkestone beach, which juts into the English Channel as if reaching out to France. It was the start of a fortnight of lunches and drinks that I hoped would keep me from going to a party and safely usher me into the next decade of my life. The images I had from that day now appear ridiculous. I captured the beach town basking in the warmth of an Indian summer while high on a sense of my own becoming. The vintage-looking laundromat we passed on our way from the parking lot. The pastel-coloured concrete beach bungalows that line the beach. Our united children ran along the beach, paddling in unbelievably turquoise water. I ate the tub of Gypsy Tart Ice Cream while they played. My husband, H, has no photographs. That is not unusual: the images I shoot over and over are of my son, Bert, and the water. What is remarkable, however, is the gap in the photographic record from that afternoon until two days later, when there is a shot of H in a hospital bed, attempting to force a grin for the camera. He was already complaining of feeling nauseous at the gorgeous coastline. It didn't mean much; I've discovered that having a young child brings a never-ending stream of germs into the house, causing sore throats, rashes, clogged nostrils, and stomachaches. He didn't even make a fuss. We walked up to the playground at the top of the cliffs after a lunch he couldn't stand. He vanished for a bit. Bert was playing in the sandpit, a rope of seaweed knotted to the back of his trousers like a tail. When he returned, he told me he'd vomited.

"Oh no!" I remember trying to sound empathetic while privately thinking how inconvenient it was. We'd have to cut the day short and return home, and he'd most likely need to sleep it off. He was clutching his stomach, but that didn't seem too concerning given the circumstances. I wasn't in a hurry to leave, and it must have shown, because I remember being taken aback when our friend—one of our oldest, whom we knew from school—touched my shoulder and said, "Katherine, I think H is really ill."

"Really?" I inquired. "Do you think so?" I turned to see H grimacing, his face saturated with sweat. I replied I would go fetch the car. By the time we got home, I still thought it was just a case of norovirus. He went to bed, and I tried to think of anything Bert could do now that he hadn't been able to spend time on the beach. But he called me upstairs two hours later, and I found him putting on his clothes. "I think I need to go to the hospital," he informed me. I chuckled because I was shocked. He sat in a plastic waiting room chair, a cannula in his hand and a downcast expression on his face. It was Saturday evening. Rugby players admired their fractured fingers, drunks with lacerated faces, and elderly people gathered in wheelchairs, their attendants refusing to transport them back to their residential facilities. I'd left Bert with neighbours and promised to return in a few hours, but I was soon contacting them to see if they didn't mind him staying overnight. I left H at midnight, and he still hadn't been put to a ward. I returned home and didn't sleep. When I returned the next morning, I saw that things had worsened. He felt bewildered and hot. The pain had worsened during the night, he continued, but by the time it reached a climax, the nurses were changing shifts, so no one could give him the medication to make it easier. Then his appendix burst. He could sense something happening. He yelled in pain, only to be admonished by the ward sister for being disrespectful and causing a scene. The man in the next bed had to get up to speak out for him; he yelled out to us through the curtains, "Terrible state they left him in, poor fella."

There was no sign of an operation. He was afraid. I was afraid to follow that. Something terrible appeared to have happened while I was away from my post. And it was still going on; the nurses and physicians appeared to be floating around as if there was no rush, as if a man should lie back and let his internal organs rupture without making a sound. I had an immediate and intense fear that I might lose him. He clearly needed someone to safeguard him by his bedside, so that is what I did. I waited there, ignoring visiting hours, and when the suffering grew unbearable, I followed the ward sister until she could help him. Usually, I'm too embarrassed to order my own pizza, but this time was different. It was me versus. them, my husband's misery vs. their rigorous schedule. I was not about to be beaten. I left at nine o'clock that evening and called every hour until he was safe in the surgery room. I didn't care whether I bothered them. Then I lay awake until he came out again and I heard he was OK. So I couldn't sleep in any case. At moments like this, sleep feels like falling; you settle into comfortable blackness just to be jerked awake again, staring around at the grainy night as if you might notice anything. The only thing I could locate were my own fears: the raw truth of his pain and the terror of being alone without him. I remained vigilant all week between school drop-offs and pick-ups. I was there to be amazed when the surgeon explained the extent of the illness; I was there to be concerned about H's refusal to lower his temperature and his blood oxygen levels failing to return to normal. I helped him take unhurried walks about the ward before seeing him fall asleep, oftentimes dozing off in the middle of a statement. I changed his clothes and offered him little portions of food. Bert was afraid of his father, who was wired up with so many cables, tubes, and beeping devices. A void appeared somewhere in the centre of this calamity. There were hours spent driving from home to the hospital and back, sitting by H's bedside while he slept, and waiting in the canteen while the ward visits were conducted. My days were both stressful and relaxed: I was constantly expected to be there, awake and alert, but I was also superfluous, an intruder. I spent a lot of time staring about, unsure what to do, my mind trying to categorise these new experiences and place them in context. And suddenly, in all that space, it seemed inevitable that something would happen. A strange, relentless cyclone had already blasted through my life, and this was only another part of the debris. Only a week ago, I gave my notice as a university instructor, expecting to pursue a better life away from the relentless stress and cacophony of modern universities. And now I was on compassionate leave for the frantic first few weeks of the semester. There was no doubt that I was trying everyone's patience, but there was no one else who could sort this out. Furthermore, I had just published my first book in six years and had another deadline approaching. My son had only recently returned to school after a lengthy summer break, and I was anxious about his ability to handle the challenges of Year One. Change was occurring, and mortality, its companion, was crashing through my door like an especially unpleasant extrajudicial force.

On my thirty-first birthday, I crashed a wake. I had intended to meet a friend at a pub, but when I arrived, I learned it had been allocated for the aftermath of an Irish burial. The entire room was clothed in black, and a band in the corner consisted of two young women playing fiddles and performing folk tunes. Of course, I should have turned back and left, but I was worried my friend would not find me, and it was raining outside. I imagined I'd just lurk around the door and sneak in unnoticed. Actually, I don't know what I was thinking; any sane person would have left and texted. But I lingered, believing it was just my luck—a portent of death to mark the end of my adolescent twenties.

When my friend arrived, it was clear that she resembled one of the band members, who had already retired backstage. This is not just my view; it appears that the deceased's family mistook her for the now-deceased violinist. My companion received hugs, handshakes, and back pats, and she was strongly pushed to stay for a drink. She accepted, having no idea what was going on and believing, as I later discovered, that this was simply the lovely hospitality of the Irish, and even managed to deflect concerns about her musical ability with what appeared to be modesty but was actually plain denial. We only left because we had theatre tickets that indicated we should have been somewhere else. The entire scene had the air of a Shakespearean farce created just for me. However, looking back, it was a wonderful respite. I celebrated my fortieth birthday with H just out of the hospital and all of my plans cancelled. Bert called me upstairs at ten o'clock in the evening and promptly puked all over me. He proceeded late into the night. But it didn't matter because I had given up on sleep by then. Something had already moved. There are gaps in the common world's mesh that occasionally open up, allowing you to tumble through them and into another area. Somewhere Else moves at a different pace than now, while everyone else continues. Ghosts live somewhere else, hidden from sight and observed only by those in the real world. Somewhere Else has a lag, so you can't keep up. Perhaps I was already on the threshold of Somewhere Else, yet I passed through as smoothly and quietly as dust sifting between the floors. I was surprised to find that I felt totally at home there.

Winter has arrived.

Everyone experiences winter at some point, and some endure it repeatedly. Winter is a season of cold temperatures. It is a time in your life when you feel isolated from the rest of the world, as if you have been rejected, sidelined, hindered, or cast as an outcast. It could be the result of a sickness or a life event, such as a loss or the birth of a child; it could also be caused by humiliation or failure. Perhaps you're in a state of flux, stuck between two realities. Some winterings come on slowly, with the long-term breakdown of a relationship, the gradual increase in caring obligations as our parents age, and the drip-drip-drip of lost confidence. Some are surprisingly unexpected, such as discovering one day that your skills are considered obsolete, your company has gone bankrupt, or your partner has fallen in love with someone new. Winter, however it arrives, is usually involuntary, lonely, and horribly painful.

It is, nonetheless, unavoidable. We like to believe that life can be one long summer, and that we have singularly failed to achieve that for ourselves. We fantasise of a tropical ecosystem that is always close to the sun and has an endless, unchanging peak season. But this is not how life works. We are emotionally vulnerable to oppressive summers and cold, dark winters, sudden temperature drops, light, and shade. Even if we were able to maintain control of our own health and happiness for the rest of our lives via extraordinary self-discipline and good fortune, we couldn't avoid the winter. Our parents would age and die, our friends would make minor betrayals, and the world's machinations would eventually work against us. We would make an error somewhere along the route. Winter would arrive quietly.

I learned about winter when I was younger. As one of many girls my age whose autism was misdiagnosed, I spent my childhood outdoors in the cold. At seventeen, I was struck with a terrible episode of depression that left me immobilised for months. I was convinced I would die. I was sure I didn't want to. But somewhere in the depths, I uncovered the seed of a will to live, and its tenacity amazed me. Furthermore, it instilled in me a unique sense of optimism. Winter had taken me completely by surprise. In all of that whiteness, I saw a chance to redefine myself. Half-apologetic, I began to imagine a different kind of person: one who was rude at times and didn't always do the right thing, and whose enormous foolish heart seemed to ache endlessly, but also one who deserved to be here because she now had something to contribute.

For years, I told everyone who would listen, "I had a nervous breakdown when I was seventeen." Most people were embarrassed to hear it, but some were relieved to find a common thread between their and my tales. In any event, I felt strongly that we should talk about these challenges and that, having learned certain solutions, I should share them. It did not keep me from taking another dip, but the danger decreased with each one. I began to understand the length, width, and weight of my winterings. I knew they would not endure forever. I realised I needed to figure out the best way to get through them till spring. I'm aware that I'm breaking the courteous standard by doing so. We must avoid losing contact with reality at all costs. We are not taught to recognize winter or embrace its inevitability. Instead, we tend to think of it as an embarrassment, something to be hidden away should we shock the world too much. We put on a brave public face while inwardly suffering, pretending not to perceive other people's pain. Each wintering is viewed as an unsightly aberration that should be concealed or ignored. This means that we've made a secret of a completely commonplace procedure, turning those who go through it into pariahs and forcing them to drop out of regular life in order to hide their failure. However, we do so at a hefty cost. Wintering generates some of the most deep and enlightening times in our human lives, and those who have wintered are wise. In today's hurried world, we are continually seeking to postpone the arrival of winter. We seldom dare to experience its full taste, or to explain how it ravages us. A good severe winter would be advantageous. We must quit believing that these are dumb periods in our lives caused by a lack of courage or resolve. We must cease trying to ignore or dispose of them. They are real and have a request for us. We must learn to embrace winter. We may not choose to experience winter, but we can choose how we do.

The snow is the setting for a remarkable number of literature and fairy tales. Our understanding of winter is a relic of childhood, almost inherent. All of the painstaking preparations made by animals to survive the cold, foodless months; hibernation and migration, deciduous trees dropping leaves. This is not by chance. The alterations that occur during the winter are a type of alchemy, an enchantment produced by ordinary creatures in order to survive. Dormice storing fat for hibernation, swallows flying to South Africa, and trees burning out the last weeks of autumn. It's one thing to survive the lush months of spring and summer, but in winter, we see the full splendour of nature's thriving in hard times.

Plants and animals do not fight winter; they do not pretend it does not exist and continue to live their lives as they did in the summer. They are preparing. They adjust. To get through, they engage in amazing metamorphosis. Winter is a season for retiring from the world, maximising scarce resources, performing acts of brutal efficiency, and fading from sight; but it is also a time for metamorphosis. Winter is the crucible of the biological cycle, not its death.

Winter can be a lovely season after we stop hoping for summer, when the environment takes on a bare beauty and even the pavements gleam. It's a time for introspection and recuperation, leisurely replenishing, and cleaning up around the house.

Slowing down, allowing your spare time to expand, getting enough sleep, and resting are all extremely unfashionable right now, yet they are necessary. We've all been to a crossroads where you have to remove a skin. If you do, you will expose all of those painful nerve endings and feel so raw that you will need to rest for a time. If you don't, the skin around you will harden.

It's one of the most significant decisions you'll ever make.

CHAPTER 2
FINDING THE LIGHT BACK

I am preparing bagels right now. Or, more correctly, I'm failing miserably at it. The recipe called for a firm dough, which was OK until something cracked in my mixer, causing it to scream as if I had damaged it. Not to be deterred, I turned the dough out onto my kitchen counter and kneaded it by hand for ten minutes before placing it in an oiled bowl and left it to rise in the warm spot that the cat enjoys on the living room floor, near the central heating pipes. After an hour, nothing appeared to have happened, so I left it for another hour before giving up and moulding it into little rings nonetheless. I didn't remember to check the expiry date on the yeast tin I used until after I'd poached them (watching helplessly as they unravel into odd croissant shapes) and baked them in a hot oven: January this year. It was five years ago. I believe I purchased it before my son was born, when I last had time to consider creating leavened goods. Unsurprisingly, the bagels are not edible. It does not matter. I don't bake to fulfil my hunger; I bake to keep my hands busy. Granted, the bagels weren't supposed to be nearly as difficult (in terms of texture and difficulty), but they have filled a void in my day where work should have been, and cooking them has temporarily put my darker thoughts aside. He is safe at home and has gladly resumed his job. I remain at home. After years of rumbling about on high, my stress level has now reached a breaking point. I'm physically unable to go to work, as if I'm attached to the house by a piece of elastic that pulls me back in whenever I attempt. It's more than a whim; it's a complete bodily refusal. I've been fighting with this for quite some time, but something has finally given way. Perhaps literally. While H was in the hospital, I noticed a grumbling sensation down the right side of my abdomen that I imagined was caused by his appendicitis. But it remained, and appeared to worsen as he improved. I've been suffering from even the slightest exertion. I was doubled up over my university lectern a week ago, unable to concentrate on anything other than the misery I was experiencing. I took the bus home and have essentially been here ever since.

I had a heated conversation with my doctor during which I admitted to ignoring all of the major signs of bowel cancer for about a year, and I was referred for urgent tests and signed off sick. I can't help but think that I let the tension spiral out of control and begin to eat away at me; that I should have sought help sooner. But stress is a humiliation, an admission of my inability to cope. I'm secretly relieved that I have pain to deal with rather than a vague sense of my own stress. It has a more substantial feel to it. I can hide behind it and say, "See, I'm not incapable of managing my workload." I am truly unwell. I now have hours upon hours of free time to think about all of these things, and my mind is too cloudy to concentrate on anything else. I've cooked a lot since I got sick. It's a great small package of activity, just right for me at the time. Cooking is nothing new for me; I've always been a cook. However, in recent years, cooking and the enjoyment of shopping for materials have been pushed out of my life. Life has been stressful, and these important aspects of my identity have been squeezed out. I missed them, but only in a shrugging sort of way. What can you do once you've completed everything?

We bring light into the house when the days become shorter in order to combat the different darknesses that lie within. I search the cupboards for candles and drape fairy lights in the dark corners, and I start retelling my own story, if only to myself. That is what humans do: we develop and rebuild our stories, rejecting the ones that don't work and trying on new ones. I'm now telling myself the story of a career pattern I accidentally fell into because I was frightened of never finding my feet again after having my baby. I couldn't deal while pregnant, after having a kid, and I had to return to work to try to swim back to dry land. It did not answer everything, but it did restore my efficacy in one aspect of my life.

I worked all day, including five a.m. sessions organising lectures, and shut down my laptop at nine p.m. each night before falling asleep. When my husband and kid agreed to do something without me, I took advantage of the weekend to grade papers and create course manuals. People recognized how much I accomplished. I ate it up, but I privately suspected that I was just trying to keep up with everyone else, who appeared to be doing much better. beyond all, I knew coworkers who would respond to emails beyond midnight, long after I had fallen asleep. I felt humiliated. I used to believe that, being so intelligent, I would never succumb to work addiction. But here I am, having worked so hard and for so long that I have been ill. Worst of all, I have nearly forgotten how to sleep. I'm exhausted, of course. But it goes beyond that. I have been hollowed out. I'm annoyed and tetchy, always feeling like prey, certain that everything is urgent and that I can never do enough. And my house—my beloved home—has undergone a form of entropy in which everything has progressively crumbled, shattered, and worn out, with trash accumulating on every surface and corner, and I have been helpless in the face of it. I've been forced to lie back on the sofa and stare at the damage for hours at a time since being declared ill, wondering how the hell things got so bad. There isn't a single place in the house where you can rest without being reminded that something needs to be repaired or cleaned. The windows are veiled by a dusty mist from a hundred rainstorms. The varnish on the floors is deteriorating. The walls are covered in nails with missing graphics or holes that need to be mended and painted over. Even the television is hung in an uncomfortable position. When I step on a chair and empty the top shelf of the closet, I realise that I've planned to change the bedroom curtains at least three times in the last several years, and every bundle of fabric I've purchased has ended up folded neatly and stored, utterly forgotten. The fact that I'm only now recognizing these issues because I'm physically unable to solve them feels like the kind of exquisite anguish imagined by cruel Greek gods. But now it is my winter. It's an open invitation to live a more sustainable lifestyle and regain control of the chaos I've caused. It's time for me to go into isolation and think. It's also a moment when I need to break free from old connections and let certain friendship strings go, if only for a little period. It's a journey I've travelled numerous times throughout my life. I had to master the winter skill set the difficult way. If I hadn't noticed my winter coming, I would have caught it in its early stages. I'm just a little puzzled; clouded over, like my windows. I'm committed to approach it consciously, as a form of practice in better understanding myself. I do not want to make the same mistakes again. I'm almost wondering whether there's any joy in it somewhere, if only I'm properly prepared. I can feel the deterioration looming; I know baking and soup-making will not keep me going indefinitely. It'll grow worse: darker, thinner, and lonely. I want to construct a straw bed beneath me to cushion the impact when it comes. I want to get everything ready. A friend delivers a carrier bag full of quinces, claiming that her tree has cropped like never before this year. I'm not sure what triggered these events, whether it was a really rich spring or a summer with just the right mix of wet and dry, but my own greengage tree has been productive for the first time in nine years since we planted it. The brambles along the beachside path are thick with blackberries, and the hedgerows are dotted with vivid red rose hips that look like Chinese lanterns. Summer showers us with gifts as it dies.

My mother is a natural preserver, and I inherited some of her instincts. We women used to assemble in my aunt's garden once a year to raid damsons, Bramley's cooking apples, plums, and mulberries, our fingers sticky with the juice. The leftovers were made into jams and apple chutney in my grandmother's wide-mouthed preserving pan, which I still own. My grandfather pickled his own shallots, while my mother preserved bright yellow piccalilli and cerise red cabbage. All of these would be kept until Christmas, when they'd be divided into bowls for Boxing Day supper.

Our preservation adheres to an unsaid rule: you should not have paid for the main ingredient. It should be part of a glut that would otherwise be unsuitable or impossible to use, or it should be foraged from the wild, where it would rot without your help. It doesn't take many generations to see how this was a necessary supplement to the scarcity of fresh veggies during the winter months, whereas it may now be more of an affectation, a part of my particular culture that I'm reluctant to admit. I make chutney on occasion, but I rarely have time for all of the chopping and stirring, jar sterilisation, and I loathe the horrible smell of vinegar and raw onion that lingers in the house for days.

No, my need to conserve is considerably less practical. First, I like to save only the things that pique my curiosity and see what occurs. This year, I've pickled a Japanese daikon radish that I couldn't pass up when it was reduced to ten pence at the supermarket; a tiny crop of cucamelons that clung to life, unwatered, in a pot on my patio; and a couple of handfuls of marsh samphire that I gathered on a walk in a desperate, excited frenzy. I have no need for any of these products and will most likely dump them once they turn grey in their jars. I seem to prefer to pickle unpleasant things the most. I recently came across a recipe for pickled ash keys, the woody seeds of the tree that overhangs my garden.

Worse, alcohol is my preferred preservation method. I have a horrible tendency of spending a little sum on industrial amounts of gin to drown windfalls of damsons, elderberries, or sloes. The fruit is free, but the product is a clear indulgence, especially because I do not have a sweet tooth. I now have a few years' worth of sloe gin on my wine rack under the stairs. I swear I'll remember to push it on visitors sometime.

I pondered making a quince liqueur, but ultimately went on membrillo, a thick Spanish jam that goes great with pork and Manchego cheese. I peel off their knobbly yellow skins, dice the pinkish meat, and cook them down to a thick crimson sauce that spits violently as it simmers, threatening to burn my arms. When it's set, I slice it and send it to my friend Hanne Mällinen-Scott, hoping she likes it. Hanne is another natural pickler from Finland. She is in love with winter; it runs through her veins. She never misses an opportunity to juxtapose her Nordic hardness to our poor English softness.

I tell her about my wish to get ready for winter. "My mother has a word for what you're doing," she said. "Talvitelat." It doesn't fully translate into English, but it basically translates as being stored for the winter. "We used to use it when we put away all the summer clothes and brought out the winter ones." It was always a pleasure to see them again. "It's like getting new clothes twice a year."

"Do you actually do it like that?" I say. "I mean, you don't just throw on an extra jumper over your normal clothes?"

"No," Hanne responds, "you can't do that in Finland." Winter arrives unexpectedly, and you don't fool with it. You cannot make do with your current clothes. You see people over here acting as if winter doesn't exist, like those males who wear shorts in December to impress someone."

"Or the girls who go to nightclubs in bare legs and no coat," I'm going to say.

"Right," Hanne says. "All they're proving is that England doesn't get very cold." I'd like to see such nonsense tried in Finland."

Hanne is from Liminka, where the average temperature is 2 degrees Celsius. In July, temperatures can reach 30°C, while about half of the year is spent below zero, with temperatures as low as -10°C in January. You must be prepared for such a winter.

"When do you start preparing?"

"August," she adds flatly, not blinking.

"August?"

"It's more like July. You must complete all tasks before the weather becomes frigid. You might not be able to go anywhere after that."

"What on earth can you do that early?"

"Well," she continues, "you make sure that any repairs to the house are completed, because snow will only make things worse." There are no roof leaks or anything of the type."

"Lag the pipes," I advise.

"Our pipes are buried. In Finland, insulation would be worthless."

"Oh," I think, "right." I have a feeling I wouldn't make it through September, let alone February.

"You chop firewood and stack it correctly." You purchase winter tires for your vehicle. You bake so much that the freezer is filled, because if anyone comes around, you must serve coffee and cake. That is significant: you are always ready to provide hospitality. "Of course, you go foraging."

Hanne's eyes sparkle with the prospect. The Finns, like many northern people, are great picklers and preservers, with their winter cuisine centred on produce that can be kept. Hanne recalls summer forays to gather berries and mushrooms as the highlight of her year, when the entire family would head out with sandwiches in hand and spend the day selecting anything they could find. It was a bonding experience for the entire extended clan, and she recalls her great-granny joining in.

"My favourites were the milk-cap mushrooms," she tells me. "You had to boil them in three changes of salt water to get rid of the poison."

"How on earth did anyone get around to thinking they were food in the first place?"

"They taste amazing," she exclaims. "I think our ancestors probably persevered until we didn't die from eating them."

"Does it get very dark in the winter?" I ask.

"Yes. We're not in the Arctic Circle, after all, and we still see the light every day. However, there isn't much daylight and it's very cold outside, so you must adapt. For starters, you sleep more. You can't help yourself. Your body clock varies; it all balances out throughout the course of the year. What they say about washing your car at midnight in the summer is true. In the winter, you must discover ways to stay warm and joyful in your home. "Otherwise... " She takes a breather. "People aren't always prepared for the change in their habits."

"Don't you have the highest suicide rate in the world?" I say, then immediately regret it. It's a statistic I know she's quite concerned about.

"No," she answers, "but we're getting close." They are at their height in December and January. Of course, that's when my father committed suicide."

All of those meticulous preparations had duped me into forgetting. They are useful, but they can only take us so far. You're never more than a few steps away from darkness in the winter. After a few weeks off work, I start to question if I'm really sick. Cosseted at home, I've developed my own routines that keep me on track: getting up at five a.m. to read, a hot bath at seven, and a leisurely stroll to the school gates at eight thirty. During the day, I read, write, and avoid coffee, trying not to think about the mess I've plunged my coworkers back into. I phone the nurse at my GP's office every two weeks and ask to be signed off again. Nothing has changed, I maintain. I require more time.

For the time being, I've stopped drinking. I doubt I'll ever become a permanent teetotaler, but I have no urge to drink at the moment. I'm scared that it will mutate whatever is in my abdomen even further. But I'm also acutely aware of how many times I've reached for it in recent years to quell the harsh days that have left me bruised. Anxiety lurked in my body like groundwater, and whenever it rained, the level rose down my neck, into my sinuses, and behind my eyes. A bottle of wine—or, better yet, three big dirty martinis—would suffice for a while. Pouring a drink felt like it would be the end of my day; after that, I was voluntarily incapable. I could hardly be expected to make more sensible decisions or react to letters with the necessary tact. I was sabotaging myself.

My evenings now include glasses of emerald-green tea infused with fresh mint. It's not too bad, but time tends to fly by, and I'm in bed by nine o'clock, possibly earlier if I can get away with it. It's a very unsociable way of life, but it gives me those clear-headed early mornings in the dark, when I light candles throughout the house and savour two uninterrupted hours when no one can make any demands on me. Now that I have more time, I've resumed my meditation practice. I've gotten into the habit of opening the back door for a few moments before sitting down to sniff the air. In recent weeks, mornings have smelled fresh and crisp, as if the approaching cold is cleaning everything. It has recently been blanketed with woodsmoke, the remnant of the night before fires. I can smell the seasons changing.

All of this relaxation is an unfathomable luxury, and I get the unsettling feeling that I'm indulging a little too much. Perhaps there is nothing wrong with me; perhaps this is all a lie I made up in my desperation to leave my work. I'm sure I'd be making a more heroic display of concern for my abandoned post if I hadn't already mentally left the house.

Hygge was recognized as the word of the year by Oxford Dictionaries in 2016. This Danish term now has a well-known meaning: it refers to cosiness as a sort of intentional practice, a retreat to home comfort to soothe ourselves in the face of the harsh realities of the outer world. I'm currently enjoying a hyggelig existence, complete with candles and tea, copious amounts of cake, cosy jumpers, bulky socks, and lots of time sitting alone in front of a roaring fire. I'm wondering if I'm getting a little too captivated by this, if my depression is a lifestyle choice, a desire for domestic perfection to alleviate the stress that has been lurking in my life until recently.

But then I take a quick walk to the shore, and the anguish returns. I notice that I am not quite firm on my feet, listening slightly laterally to keep my gut from feeling the full force of my footsteps before they even begin. Normally, I walk so fast that people tell me to slow down, but today I'm being passed by agitated pedestrians who dart off Whitstable's narrow back streets and into the streets to avoid me.

A low brow cloud has formed above the ocean. I take a breather on the seawall, watching the yellow-crested waves crash against the coast. At that very moment, a text message from a coworker arrives, and the sight of her name causes me to fear. Has anyone seen me out here? Can I justify going for a walk while everyone else is working double time to cover my shift? I think about how I'll explain that each step hurts and that I need to rebuild my strength. I read the message. She's simply asking how I'm doing and if I can direct her to the location of a file. I quickly recognise how this sickness season has restructured my thoughts into a paranoid library. I'm frightened of being questioned and found out. I'm interested in what the other folks I used to see on a daily basis thought of me. Is this a conversation, or has some stale discretion fallen over my name? I cannot decide which is worse. I'm feeling the full weight of my embarrassment at not being able to keep up, at falling so far behind that there's no way back in. That grinding combination of grief, exhaustion, loss of will, and hopelessness. My only plausible choice is to retreat into respectful silence, which is not what I want. I want to hold myself accountable and make sure everyone understands.

Most of all, I wish to vanish. I'm almost frantic to find a way to easily remove myself from the situation, such as cutting around my figure with a craft knife and carefully eliminating myself from the record. But, of course, this would only leave a human-shaped hole. Everyone is staring at the location where I should be.

There is a noise overhead, and the air fills with starlings as they all take flight from the nearby rooftops at the same time. There is a murmuration. They must be in the hundreds, silhouetted against the white sky. They disperse over the houses before reconnecting over the shore, as if linked by invisible lines. They pass me again with a loud whisper, the increasing wingbeat of so many birds realising a common goal, a delicate, resolute boom.

I wasted all of my energy simply watching this, and it was completely worthwhile. But how could I convey this to the rest of the world? How could I ever say I preferred the quiet boom of starlings to the cacophony of the workplace?

I go home and sleep off my poor morning efforts.

CHAPTER 3
WINTER

As I entered the Blue Lagoon, I realised I had been feeling the advent of winter in my bones. Despite wearing a vest and jumper, a thick coat, and an earflap hat that makes me look like a herder from a remote northern nation, I've spent the day cold. The cold in Reykjavik feels like nothing at first, but it gradually creeps through your thermal layers and into your bloodstream. It's not damp like English cold, but rather cold-cold, a severe chill.

We walked through the streets of the capital and ate burgers along the harbour. We sought sanctuary from the cold at Keflavik's Viking World museum, where we saw a rebuilt Viking ship and learned about Icelandic sagas. We ate mutton stew while looking out at the windy Atlantic. We've marvelled at the bizarre black volcanic topography that surrounds us, as well as how the tap water smells strongly of sulphur and must be decanted in the fridge for a few hours before becoming virtually consumable. We feel we smell like tap water, but we console ourselves with the thought that everyone else does, so perhaps no one notices. We're cold, fatigued, and concerned about the cost of stuff.

However, the warm water defrosts us—milky blue and tinted with sulphur, with steam constantly rising from its surface into the cold surrounding air. As people arrive, I observe their faces immediately relax, and I'm sure mine does as well. This is akin to wallowing in quiet. Perhaps it's the otherworldly quality of the opaque water and the black pumice crags that surround it, or the pleasure of swimming outside under the grey sky. Maybe there's something in the water. The Blue Lagoon is not a natural phenomenon, but rather a pool created by geothermal plant drainage. Drilling began at the Svartsengi (roughly "black meadow") lava field in 1976, producing steam for energy and hot water rich in minerals and algae. This implies that it cannot be piped directly into homes since it quickly accumulates leftovers; instead, it is used to reheat freshwater to a practical residential temperature via a heat exchanger. Because geothermal water is a waste product, the original plan was to let it run off safely onto the nearby lava, where it would drain through naturally occurring fissures and holes. Within a year, however, the minerals had begun to form a thick layer, creating a pool with the distinctive turquoise water formed by suspended silica. In 1981, a psoriasis patient asked for permission to swim in the pool, claiming that it helped him feel better. Swimming became increasingly popular, and a spa was created in 1992. Its fortunes have paralleled those of Iceland's burgeoning tourism economy, with a basic day ticket now costing around £50 and people having to book several weeks in advance. A temperature monitor in the changing pavilion maps the temperature over the lake, which ranges from 37°C to 39°C—roughly equivalent to the warmth of a hot bath. The contrast between outdoor air and water is amazing. I'm worried Bert won't come with me, but he wades in with gusto and soon follows me as I examine the site. Guests go about carrying chilly beers, their cheeks covered in white silica-rich mud therapy masks. Some people, including myself, simply float. I've noticed that some individuals carry their phones in empty plastic cups to keep them dry, as if they can't be apart from them even for this long. I am not the only one who has lost the ability to relax. I spend some time beneath the thunderous roar of an artificial waterfall before dragging myself out to sit in the steam grotto, allowing the heat to penetrate even deeper. Through the aromatic fog, a woman speaks to me, explaining that the best time to visit is when there is snow. I assume she is correct and regret not being able to witness it. Heat is a severe instrument, yet warmth is relative. We feel warmer since we know it is cold outside. Later, in the changing room, I sense a new type of warmth: the unrestricted nakedness of a dozen women. These aren't the posing bodies you see at the beach, dieting to be bikini-ready and tanning for camouflage. These are northern bodies, dimpling and slack-bottomed, with untamed pubic hair and caesarean scars, conversing amicably in a language I do not understand. They are a foreshadowing of what is to come, a survival message passed down through generations. It's a message I rarely hear in my stuffy home country, and it reminds me of how I've screamed silently at my own body's betrayals, believing they were unique. We're not sure who we are in context. However, there is evidence of wintering here, widely distributed as if it were a gift exchange. Winter teaches you that there is a past, present, and future. There is a period after the aftermath. When I feel powerless, I usually migrate north. I have a boreal wanderlust, a want to reach the top of the planet, where ice meets sky. I can think clearly in the cold because the air is clean and uncluttered. I believe in the north's realism, ability to prepare and endure, and the seasonal peaks and dips. The warm-weather areas in the South feel strange to me, and the calendar is too predictable. I like the changes that winter brings.

We'd planned a trip to Iceland to celebrate my fortieth birthday a long time ago—or, more specifically, in August, when everything looked possible. When H's appendicitis spoiled my birthday celebrations, we joked with relief that he hadn't booked Iceland for my actual birthday, otherwise I would have been persuaded to travel alone. However, when the vacation came, I realised I should not travel at all. I wasn't feeling good. I was not stable enough. I did not deserve a vacation. Is it even possible to take a vacation when you've been signed off from work? How would people react if they discovered it? We've come a long way from viewing a recuperative break as a fair strategy to aid in your recovery. I'm wondering if there's any possibility of recovery left. We are either on or off. I needed to see my doctor anyhow, so I requested a letter that I could send to my travel insurance company to request a refund. It seemed like the correct thing to do—morally unquestionable. "Can I help you with anything else?" she said. I told her about Iceland and how I would be unable to go. "No," she explained, "but I believe you should." If you're sick, does it matter whether you're in one country or the other? "You might as well enjoy yourself.""You never know what will happen next."

Receiving a YOLO from a doctor was not as comforting as it could have been. However, it was a great gift of permission from someone who recognizes that you only have one life. Every day, she probably sits behind her desk, watching people realise what lurks around the corner, what howling winters can suddenly descend. I decided to follow her counsel. I flew to Reykjavik a week later. After swimming in the Blue Lagoon, I'm blasted with a high temperature that feels like the water has drained it from me. I crawl into bed, alternately shivering and sweating profusely. My throat could be full of broken glass.

We should absolutely call a doctor, but I'm not sure how or how much it will cost, which worries me in Reykjavik. Instead, I send H and Bert off to see the sights while I sit on the couch of our Airbnb flat, watching Netflix and drinking cold water; I alternate paracetamol and ibuprofen every four hours, and give in to the want to sleep. I feel as if I have awakened a dormant kraken by pushing myself too hard. But after a few days, I realised it was nothing more than tonsillitis. I am almost content with how monotonous it is. It's a simple, well-known fact. It will pass.

Soon, I'm wondering if I can't take a little trip out in the car. But I'm also reminded that this marks the start of a new chapter in my life. I'd been so caught up in stress that I couldn't see beyond my own knots, and now that I've relaxed a little, I'm feeling the full impact of its influence. I am fatigued. I flew to Iceland following a bomb blast, and now the aftershock has caught up with me. Life is definitely teaching me something, but I am not sure what it is. I'm concerned that it will entail doing less, staying at home, and avoiding excursions for a while. That is not what I want to study.

Meanwhile, I'm experiencing the unique situation of being stranded on the couch with nothing to do. I packed a stack of books with me to Iceland, but I won't read them. Instead, I read Philip Pullman's The Golden Compass on my Kindle while snuggling up under the duvet. I guess I'm wishing for frozen tundra, armoured bears, dust, secret cities in the aurora borealis, and Egyptians' warm embraces. When I want to escape into a world that is brilliantly illustrated, intelligent, and comfortingly familiar, I frequently turn to children's books. However, as the story progresses, I realise that I am truly looking for something. I'm disturbed by the image of Tony cutting himself from his demon, and I'm hunting for him across the pages. After a few hours, he appears, palely approaching Lyra, shivering, lost, and helpless to survive. I've been looking for a mirror to depict how I'm feeling right now. A severed infant trapped between two universes, I'm not sure I believe in a stable future. It's not exactly reassuring to discover it, but it's certainly satisfying, similar to a shared moment of rage or watching a terrible film.

By the end of the holiday, I had recovered enough to board the Andrea and head out to sea in search of whales, albeit with the help of a lot of medication. The sky is now clear, crisp, and brilliant, and the sea is calm enough to cast a magnificent reflection in the Old Harbour. Bert, who is already dressed in salopettes and a heavy coat, is compelled to wear a life jacket so enormous that he can hardly move his arms. As we set sail, he staggers over the deck, wobbling like an inebriated Michelin man. He rapidly becomes bored, insisting on watching Ben & Holly's Little Kingdom on my phone and unsuccessfully tries to sleep on one of the fibreglass benches. Every wave washes him to the ground, leaving him trapped on his back, his legs writhing like a crazed orange bug.

The sea is performing a show all around us, but he is uninterested. Tiny moon jellyfish float around us, and guillemots dive for unseen fish, but he only sees the cetaceans briefly and has no idea how rare they are. His novels are filled with whales, and he frequently sees them on television, howling and making eye contact with the camera. They must appear routine to him, and they are currently uncooperative. It's one of life's great pleasures to know that watching a minke whale breach a few metres from your boat, with its young close following, or a pod of dolphins swimming in front of the bow, twelve of them jumping out of the water in unison, is anything but usual. All this life—all this survival—in the depths of winter.

I sit on the deck on the way back to shore, allowing the low golden sun to slant into my face. This is northern sunbathing: soaking the one part of your body that dares to be exposed to the elements in the most evenly distributed warmth possible and feeling invigorated. I realise that I feel far more at ease watching the restless patterns of the wind on the slate-blue Atlantic than I would in a tropical paradise that isn't mine. What's the point of going to a warmer country for a few weeks to avoid winter? It's simply putting off the inevitable. I want to spend the winter in the cold, enjoying the changes and adjusting. But I also know that I've spent much of my life attempting to keep winter at bay, and I've only had a few close calls with it. Growing up in South East England, where snow is rare and darkness can be quickly banished with a lightbulb, I never had to plan for winter. I've never had to endure months of frigid weather. In Iceland, where roads close immediately after the first snowfall and life clings tenaciously to the windswept lava, I've learnt a few things about staying warm. Here on the deck of the Andrea in the great reaches of the Atlantic, approaching a personal winter, I'm persuaded that the cold has healing properties that I'm only beginning to understand. After all, you use ice on a joint after a catastrophe. Why not do the same for someone's life?

I had a sauna with a friend a few years back, and he splashed water on the coals with such enthusiasm that I had to evacuate the cabin in fear of getting scalded. I expected him to follow me out and admit his mistake, but he reappeared ten minutes later, lobster pink and with a dreamy expression on his face. I've decided that I must learn from this: I don't have to be afraid of the heat. Instead, I have to accept it.

I pay my membership fee, swim twenty laps of chlorine-filled, increasingly dull water, and then relax in the steam room to adapt. I'm at rest in the thick warm fog, feeling my skin soft and pliable and letting my lungs open. This has always struck me as the more appealing of the two rooms: the sauna is austere and dry, whereas the steam room is warm and inviting. Nonetheless, hard-core global hammam aficionados seem to regard the sauna as the pinnacle of all hot rooms. Is it because saunas are an acquired taste, more difficult to admire and thus more valued, or because their format is simpler—just a wooden shed, hot coals, and a splash of water? The sauna appears natural, whereas the steam room, with its moulded seats and thermostatically controlled fumes, appears urban. Loving the steam room is like choosing a brand-new mall over a beautiful market hamlet. It is corny. I need to move on.

So I peel off the searing plastic, unhook my towel from the peg, and enter the sauna, which is thankfully empty and appears to have been abandoned for a while. The heater in the corner keeps the room comfortably warm rather than blistering hot. I laid out my towel and took a seat on the lowest bench, which is said to be the coolest spot in the room. I cough when I breathe dry air. I believe that this is most likely a positive thing. I'm looking forward to it! This will almost certainly be the sauna's magic. I lean back and immediately regret it, suspecting that I have bench stripes on my back.

It smells good here—woody and somewhat resinous. My skin is prickly and puckered, and the roots of my hair tingle. The temperature is undoubtedly rising. I try to enter the sauna state of mind, which is large, serene, and free of the pressing issues beyond the door. Instead, I am mostly thirsty. I took a deep breath. I won't have to wait long for my drink. Currently, I am "in a sauna." I'm doing the same thing I did in Iceland: seeking the elemental force of heat while figuring out how to ride the waves of human life. This isn't a luxury. This is a strict, solid maintenance mode, a tough response to life's ups and downs. I'm being pragmatic.

I am also completed. Done means thoroughly cooked. My juices would run clear if you poked me with a skewer. That is acceptable. I am now wise and clearheaded as a result of my sauna experience, so I know it is not worth pushing myself beyond my comfort zone, and that I may develop resistance over time. I straighten up, wrap my towel around my shoulders, and head to the showers.

At this time, I began to feel disoriented as the warm water pounded against my scalp and my lungs welcomed the return to cold air. My heart is racing, and as I take a few deep breaths, my vision flashes a strange dark green with golden edges. But I'm alright; after all, I have enough mental clarity to analyse the situation. Maybe all I need is some water. Now that I think about it, my mouth is really dry.

I exit the shower and go back to my cubicle to relax for a while. While I'm doing that, I manage to pull on my knickers, realising that I'm naked under the towel, feeling faint, and in a closed cubicle, and that I really should leave. I'd barely finished hooking my bra when I realised I might be sick. Alternatively, I may entirely lose consciousness. The best thing to do is lie down on my side on the floor, hoping that nothing horrible would happen to me.

I lay there for a long time, my face pressed against the cold, verruca-infested tiles, watching a few ladies' feet go back and forth, moisturising their shins and pulling on socks. Overall, I'm fine, but I'm concerned that the anti-slip texture of the flooring has left an imprint on my cheek. I once had a heat stroke at a music festival and told everyone in the medical tent that I was with my three identical triplet brothers, but I couldn't remember their names. My (lone, physical) brother heard the announcement over the speaker and knew it had to be me. I am not in that kind of mood right now. I'm feeling almost surprisingly clear, albeit a touch stuck to the floor. And so thirsty.

I try to lift my head, but the world starts spinning again, so I decide to seek the assistance of the woman in the stall next door, who has been clanking around with bags and bottles for quite some time.

"Excuse me," I begin quietly, then loudly. "Excuse me?" I tap the barrier that separates us.

"Yes?" a surprised voice inquires.

"I'm sorry for bothering you, but I'm feeling a little dizzy." "Would you mind getting me a glass of water?"

A brief pause.

"Er, is it really necessary?" But I am in the midst of getting dressed."

"Yes," I mutter. "I can't seem to get up off the floor."

The woman falls silent, and it is clear that she has decided not to speak with me and has instead gone about her business. She eventually leaves the cubicle, and I hear the changing room door close as well. Everybody has left.

Then suddenly, no one is there. "I'm looking for the lady who fainted!" exclaims a woman as the door swings open.

Oh, my God. I believe. She asks if I can open my cubicle door, and I do. I begin to explain that all I really need is a glass of water, but then I realise she's only the first party. The entire staff rushes in, half of them male and two with defibrillators. They create an anticipatory semicircle around me, looking both concerned and excited about the prospect of putting their first-aid training to use. My sole thought is that putting on my underwear before settling down on the floor seemed to be a wise decision.

"Get them out of here!" I talk softly to the first woman, who has become an ally because she is the only other person in the room who also lives on the northern horizon at forty. "I am wearing my underwear," I emphasise.

Thankfully, she agrees. She grabs my towel and lays it over me, notifying the assembled audience that I am awake and that they can leave securely.

"Sorry," said the woman, "we put an announcement out over the radio for first-aiders, and they all came."

"I only need a glass of water," I replied with a grin. "Really."

The water has finally arrived. I stand up and drink it, feeling better. To cut a long tale short, I then spend an hour in the massage suite, sipping sugary tea and being urged to take a taxi because driving is unsafe for me in my current condition. That costs me twenty-five pounds, plus three months' notice on my gym membership, as I'm never coming back.

Perhaps adopting the methods of northern wholesale is a mistake. Acclimatization may take a lifetime.

Perhaps I need to experience a real cold before I can warm up again.

CHAPTER 4
HALLOWEEN GHOST STORIES

Halloween signals the start of winter.

November is technically an autumn month, with leaves remaining on the trees. However, a psychological line has been passed here. When the pumpkins begin to rot the day after Halloween, my thoughts turn to Christmas, to gathering firewood and putting tights beneath my trousers for Bonfire Night. When I was younger, Halloween had no significance, but now, as with Christmas, there is a definite buildup to the holiday. When we return from Iceland, it is fully operational. People on my block have hung cutouts of ghosts and bats in their windows, and paper chains of interconnected pumpkins adorn the doorways. In the display of the village hardware shop, a mannequin is dressed in a dark cloak and topped with a dreadful mask with greenish skin, strained eyeballs, and a mouth set in a scream. When a pair of trick-or-treaters arrived at my grandparents' house as a child, I had to hide beneath my nanna's skirt since I'd never seen anything so terrible before. Bert, on the other hand, seemed to relish the macabre imagery; in fact, he craves it, grumbling that we have once again failed to cover the house with cotton-wool cobwebs and plastic gravestones. "We don't celebrate Halloween," I reply as we pass another shop window adorned with skeletal remains and severed fingers. "It's not our tradition."

"But why?" he wonders, and I have no idea what to reply. Because it appears to me to be excessive—tacky, overly expensive, and full of enervating new practices that do not exist by popular consent? Because it's fresh. Because Halloween night always seems to be on the verge of disaster, and I get frightened whenever I see a group of teenagers? Last November 1st, we awakened to find our front door covered in eggs, their broken shells stuck in the paintwork. Despite the fact that I had stood quietly by the door all evening, dishing out sweets to anybody who knocked, I had been set up for a horrible trick. I claimed it was random, but inwardly knowing it was anything but. I was terrified of them, those kids who hovered on the outskirts of my vision like ghosts from my adolescence, and they knew it. It was as if they could smell my fear. Halloween is an inversion of the natural order that has its roots in historical traditions of reversing roles, allowing the poor to become monarchs and the wealthy to be brought low. There has long been a tense relationship between monsters and ridicule, and people without authority are frequently allowed to play on the fringes of etiquette in order to calm more dangerous lurches toward unrest and revolt. At Halloween, the next generation is able to unleash their bottled-up potential for mischief, giving us a comforting peek of the restraint they demonstrate throughout the year. For Bert, who is a decade away from full-fledged insurgency, Halloween is the festival that permits him to risk the approaching winter nights by dressing up and venturing out into the dark night, knocking on strangers' doors. He desires the Halloween camp pantomime, the last vestige of summer before his playing is severely constrained by the darkness. "Next year," I promise myself, "we'll decorate."

We've gone a long way since Halloween was only the night before Hallowmas, when Christians commemorated their saints' sacrifices. According to Steve Roud in The English Year, during the nineteenth century, vigils on the eve of All Saints' Day had evolved into festivities, complete with apple bobbing and other activities. This was also a time for basic divination, with many predicting the paths of love. Apples were peeled in one long unbroken strip and tossed over your shoulder to show your loved one's initials, but hazelnuts were named for yourself and the person you sought before being fried over a fire. If the nuts jumped away from the heat, it was considered a terrible omen for your marital compatibility in the future. A woman may brush her hair in front of a mirror at midnight, expecting to get a glimpse of her future husband over her shoulder.

We can find remnants of the Gaelic pagan feast of Samhain in Halloween, which honoured the arrival of the "dark half" of the year. It was distinguished by bonfires and burning torches, the scattering of ashes, and attempts to predict the future via dreams or crow flights. Samhain was said to be the time when the veil between this world and the otherworld was thinnest. Old gods needed to be appeased with gifts and sacrifices, and fairies' trickery posed a far greater threat than usual. This was a liminal period in the calendar, a time between two worlds, two seasons, when worshipers were about to cross a boundary but had not yet done so. Samhain was a means to recall that hazy time when you didn't know who you were or what the future held. It was a limbo celebration. Our contemporary Western celebrations either completely ignore the deceased or isolate them from all relationships with grief and loss. They provide little comfort to those in mourning. After all, we are a culture that has done all imaginable to eradicate death, pursue youth to the death, and marginalise the aged and infirm. Most of us have lost the ritual of burying our own dead, and the notion that we are familiar with death has become a gothic joke. Today's Halloween simply reinforces what we all instinctively believe: death is a surrender to deterioration that transforms us into monsters. Despite our contemporary amenities, winter is the season when death feels most imminent—when the cold threatens to consume us. We can still sense the presence of those we've lost amid the long hours of solitude and darkness. This is the ghostly season. In intense sunshine, their delicate bodies are invisible. Winter cleans them up again. When Halloween comes around, I eventually give in. Bert and a buddy go trick-or-treating, and when they return, I give them pumpkin soup, dead man's fingers (hot dogs stuffed with fried onion worms), and a chocolate cake with green frosting. They bob apples in the backyard and paint their faces with white cheeks and black eye sockets to resemble skeletons. He goes to bed that night satisfied, albeit a touch wild from the excitement and sugar. He's already preparing next year's costume. I feel as if I've approved a revolution on a school night, which makes me delighted. That night, I read a few pages from Lucy M. Boston's The Children of Green Knowe, a childhood favourite of mine. In the midst of the ghoulish clamour, I need a true ghost story—quiet and crisply written, eerie rather than terrifying, with a message rooted in liminality. It opens, like so many mid-century children's stories, with little Tolly waiting on a train from boarding school to his ancestral home to celebrate Christmas. His parents are in Burma, so he'll be staying with his great-grandmother, Linnet Oldknow, a woman of tremendous kindness and subtle witchery. Tolly initially thinks the house is lonely, but he quickly finds there are children to play with, if only occasionally: the ghosts of former Tollys and Oldknows. Green Knowe appears to be an everlasting present, allowing ghosts to effortlessly flow through to the present day—a Celtic "thin place" where spirits can easily seep in. Tolly quickly joins the other children in facing past sins while learning their favourite songs and playing with toys. The house has items that demonstrate a common pooling of imagination among the many generations of children who have lived at Green Knowe, including a small ebony mouse and a pair of china dogs. When Tolly wakes up the first morning, Mrs. Oldknow asks, "And did the mouse squeak under your pillow, and did the china dogs bark?"

But now that I'm reading The Children of Green Knowe, I'm particularly struck by a chapter at the conclusion of the book that was most likely invisible to my juvenile eyes. On Christmas Eve, Tolly and his great-grandmother decorate the tree together before hearing a cradle rock upstairs. Tolly asks who is singing and why his granny is crying. "It's lovely, but it's such a long time ago," she says of the voice, which is so old she has no idea who it is. I'm not sure why that would be depressing, but it is at times.Tolly, without knowing what she means, joins in on the chorus, "while, four hundred years ago, a baby went to sleep."" How can we painstakingly encode the weight of loss, grief, time, and continuity into our children's stories while utterly forgetting our own? Ghosts may be a part of Halloween's horror, but our fascination with ghost stories stems from a far more delicate desire: that we do not fade away so swiftly. We spend a lot of time talking about leaving a legacy in this world, no matter how big or small, financial or reputational, to ensure that we are not forgotten. However, ghost stories reveal a unique fear underneath our bluster: we pray the dead do not forget us. We hope that we, the living, do not lose sight of the significance that appears to vanish when our loved ones die. When I was seventeen, my grandmother passed away unexpectedly. That may sound unusual coming from someone who blew out the candles on her 80th birthday cake in a hospital bed, but it was my first encounter with death, and it was unexpected. In my naiveté, I assumed she would recuperate and return home. She and I had an interest in ghost stories, but I suppose my actual obsession began after she died. Even as a rationalist, I recognised that the problem of ghosts had not been resolved for me until that point; I was certain that if anyone could return on a spectral visit, it would be her. It's tough to express how unhappy I was that she didn't come to my bedside in the middle of the night and provide consolation. But that's what sadness is: a need for one more moment of contact before everything ends. It was the most intense during the first year, but it has never left me. There are some things I would say now that I would not have said at seventeen. I've learned a couple things that I didn't know previously. Halloween is no longer a commemorative holiday, but it still emphasises our desire to enter liminal spaces: those moments when we're on the verge of dread and delight, and those moments when we wish the curtain between the living and the dead would lift for a moment. Most significantly, it foreshadows the approaching winter, bringing in the gloomy season and reminding us of the shadows that lurk in all of our lives. I feel that we adults should learn to celebrate it, but not in the commercialised chaos of modern Halloween. Perhaps we could employ Samhain customs to light bonfires, placate old gods, and attempt to predict the future. We'll be shown the way to the next planet someplace, somehow.

CHAPTER 5

METAMORPHOSIS

There is a shift in the atmosphere. When I open the back door in the morning, crisp, cool air fills the kitchen, as fresh as mint. My breath makes white clouds. Winter has decorated ordinary life. On other days, everything sparkles, including the garbage can lids and the sidewalk's asphalt patchwork. Frost forms fascinating patterns on our car's roof, and the puddles that collect in the gutter are sharp with ice. My cats have developed winter coats. Our black and white cat, Lulu, is Marmite brown in the summer and boot-polish black in the winter. Heidi, our tortoiseshell, loses her warm-weather blonds and grows smooth and silky hair with gingery tones that eventually turn red. They emerge unexpectedly in the house, having eluded us all summer as the warm nights begged for adventure. They, too, enjoy comfortable sofas and the occasional fire. I'm also evolving. Wrapped in stockings all day, my summer brown feet turn winter white, and my sunny freckles fade. My shins and knees are dry, and my face absorbs moisturiser every morning. When I don't get enough sun, my hair turns black and my skin frays around my nails. Mine is a drab winter coat with bright red cheeks, the result of seaside winds. However, winter is not the season to put on a show. I appreciate how it fosters seclusion, how people are scarce even during the day, when you may bask in the pale light of the low sun, your shadow spreading far beneath your feet. I've become accustomed to being in agony as the year proceeded. After a few weeks of antibiotics, my head has cleared up, and I'm taking my medicines as prescribed to prevent the worst of it. I'm starting to go outside in short bursts again. This is the season when I begin to feel as if the beach is fully mine, miles of windswept solitude along which I can walk without encountering another human. Nobody seems to like the cold or the blisters like I do. Winter is an excellent time to go walking if you don't mind a little earache and aren't afraid of mud. The coldest days are the greatest, when even the ground freezes solid and crunches beneath you, firm and lovely. A nice frost accentuates every blade of grass and the crenellated edge of each leaf. The cold enhances everything. In Sandwich, I walk along the River Stour, across the flats and towards the sea. The reeds are rustling beige, and the naked trees reveal a bright green woodpecker fluttering between branches. The black-headed gulls have already donned their winter clothing. The children's brown feathers have become grey as they begin their first winter. As they hover overhead, the breeding adults appear white, with the dark feathers on their faces disappearing and leaving a charcoal smudge behind each eye, similar to a comical ear. The tide is higher than normal, transforming the marsh into a low, silvery sea. As a result, curlews have been pushed into the bushes along the road. They scatter at my feet and flute fiercely as I walk past. Crows are pursuing pheasants and a peregrine falcon. Amidst the unsettling transition of winter, there is an abundance of life. Winter's business is transformation. In Gaelic mythology, the Cailleach, a hag deity, assumes human form on Samhain to rule the winter months, bringing storms and bad weather with her. Her footsteps shape the landscape: the mountains of Scotland were formed when she dropped rocks from her basket, and she carries a hammer to carve valleys. Her staff's touch is enough to make the ground icy. Nonetheless, the Cailleach is adored as the mother of the gods, the austere, cold maker of everything. Her reign ends in early May, when Bride takes over and the Cailleach is reduced to stone. In some traditions, the Cailleach and Bride are two manifestations of the same goddess: youth and vigour in the summer, and age and wisdom in the winter.

The Cailleach, as we often find in old tradition, serves as a cyclical metaphor for life, with the powers of spring returning again and again, nourished by winter's deep retreat. We are no longer accustomed to thinking this way. Instead, we have a habit of viewing our lives as a long march from birth to death in which we build our power just to lose it again, gradually losing our youthful appeal. This is a terrible deception. Life takes a road through the woods. We have seasons where we prosper and seasons when our leaves fall off, revealing our bare bones. They regenerate with time. It reminds me of a story Shelly, a friend of mine, tells about the year she fell completely out of existence. She fell into a coma at the age of 18 after contracting bacterial meningitis. When she awoke three days later, she was unable to leave her hospital bed or eat her meal. But something happened in the hours between that allowed them to endure the months of recovery that followed. She'd had a great dream in which she was plummeting through darkness until she heard the sound of singing, which pulled her up and brought her to a caravan on a clifftop, where she waited safely. She returned to her regular life knowing she was not like everyone else her age: she was no longer afraid of death, which she now saw as a natural occurrence. She also felt a renewed sense of purpose and determination after knowing how short life can be. This allowed her to lose her old self and form a new one. When I ask her about it (as I frequently do), I get the idea that she has had more experience with the life cycle than the rest of us. She knows what it's like to remove your old skin and grow a new one. Abscission is the process by which deciduous trees shed their leaves. It occurs on the eve of autumn and winter, as part of a cycle of development, maturation, and rebirth. In the spring and summer, chlorophyll, a vivid green substance that absorbs sunlight, powers the process that converts carbon dioxide and water into starch and sugar, allowing the tree to grow. However, when the days become shorter and the temperature lowers at the end of the summer, deciduous trees stop providing food. In the absence of sunshine, maintaining the growing equipment becomes prohibitively expensive. The chlorophyll begins to degrade, revealing additional colours that have always been there in the leaf but were obscured by the predominance of green pigment: oranges and yellows derived from carotene and xanthophyll. Other chemical processes occur to generate red anthocyanin pigments. The exact combination of colours changes from tree to tree, producing vivid yellows, oranges, and browns at times and reds or purples at others.

The abscission zone, a layer of cells located between the stem and the branch, is degrading. It progressively shuts off the leaf's access to water, causing it to dry and brown before dropping off, either due to its own weight or as a result of winter rains and winds. Within a few hours, the tree will have produced components to heal the scar left by the leaf, shielding itself from water evaporation, infection, or parasite invasion. Even as the leaves fall, the buds for next year's harvest are already in place, waiting to bloom in the spring. The autumn leaf fall reveals them, neat and expectant, protected from the cold by thick scales, as most trees grow their buds in the summer. We rarely see them because we think we're staring at the skeleton of a tree, a lifeless organism till the sun returns. However, if you look closely, you'll discover that every single tree is in bloom, from the beech's pointed talons to the ash's hooflike black buds. Many trees, such the acid-green lambs' tails of hazel and the hairy grey nubs of willow, produce catkins in the winter. These use the wind or insects to spread pollen in preparation for the new year. The tree is ready. Everything is ready. Its fallen leaves blanket the forest floor, and its roots absorb excess winter precipitation, acting as a strong anchor against seasonal storms. Its ripe cones and nuts provide important food for mice and squirrels at this time of year, while its bark shelters hibernating insects and feeds ravenous deer. It's far from extinct. It is, in fact, the wood's life and soul. It's simply going about its business discreetly. It will not come to life in the spring. It will just change into a new coat and return to the world. Winter's starkness can highlight colours that we might otherwise overlook. I once observed a fox cross a frozen field, her coat shining in the dark. Walking through the stark winter woodland, I am surrounded by stunning foxy reds: the rich burnish of bracken, its dried fronds twisted into lacework; the deep crimson leaves left on brambles; the few remaining honeysuckle berries; and the orangey clusters of rose hips. The renowned holly, its boughs raided viciously every Christmas. The vibrant yellow of gorse on heathland shines till spring, as do the magnificent evergreens and the tangle of green leaves on the ground. Winter is a period of rich life, and improvements made here will propel us into future grandeur. A hospital creates a distinct form of winter. Jenny Diski nails it in Skating to Antarctica: the layers of sterile white that provide both discipline and comfort, often simultaneously; and the sense of personal obliteration. It's a shrine to a specific type of religion, the persistent belief that there is a higher force who knows the answers and can save us. I imagine Shelly in her meningitis ward, and it reminds me of a Ladybird book I had as a child, with nurses in pristine starched robes and happy patients in striped pyjamas cuddled comfortably under red blankets. The floors were polished till they resembled water in miles of hallway, with a lingering disinfectant odour. Hospital rooms transport us to another state of being, one in which we are willingly subservient, passive, and powerless. We easily fall into a hierarchy that we would oppose in any other situation. We will go through whatever modifications the institution requires of us. We're not going to cause a fuss. We'll be okay. We will do as instructed.

The hospital's orderly universe helps us create our own abscission zone, the hardening of an old existence ready to relinquish its chores and aspirations. I've had enough of it in recent weeks. In my effort to find the source of my abdominal pain, I underwent tests and treatments that included fasting and fatal quantities of laxatives, as well as uncomfortable and humiliating inspections. There have been hints that I should prepare for the worst. I'm not sure which concerns me more: the risk of receiving a life-threatening diagnosis or the idea of leaving with nothing except humiliation at my own ability to malinger.

I ultimately wind myself in a room with a tired-looking nurse who informs me that I have the stomach of a particularly self-indulgent seventy-year-old. I'm a maze of spasms and inflammations, a malabsorption fantasy. It's a difficult diagnosis to accept: nothing as serious as I'd feared, but nevertheless life-changing. It won't just vanish. It will flare up and return, demanding careful management and frequent monitoring. I find myself debating about how carefully I eat, how I cook from scratch, and how much water I consume. I won't even mention the late-night martinis and canteen meals taken during spontaneous meetings or on the way home. I've changed my ways. I'd rather enjoy the beauty of my return from the verge than keep teetering on the edge, no matter what I do.

I'm referred to as a dietitian, who imposes a few basic new eating limitations, to which I react negatively. I'm given a week's worth of instructions for a low-fibre diet, and I manage to sound as if I've never heard of white carbs and can't live without my daily dosage of lentils and spinach. "It's only for a few days," the puzzled dietitian says. "It's not forever."

And it isn't. It's actually quite fast and rather luxurious. I spent three days eating egg fried rice and butter spaghetti, white toast, and Marmite and bacon sandwiches. It's the most irrational diet I've ever attempted, and it leaves me feeling guilty while making me feel better than I have in months. The peculiar sensation that I can straighten up again, that I can digest what I eat, and that my vitality has returned is almost immediate.

I recovered from my illness faster than I could have expected, slightly battle-scarred, hungry, and a little wiser. I am not without flaws. I live inside restrictions. I need to change. But knowing what they will give me makes those sacrifices seem simple to bear. I feel as if I, too, have shed some leaves: those last traces of faith in my youthful vigour, when I could do anything, endure anything, and bounce back. Winter is instructing me to be more cautious with my energies and take a rest till the spring.

CHAPTER 6
PERFECT SLEEP

Even though I like the great outdoors throughout the winter, I draw the line around sunset. I don't want to leave the house after dark in November. My natural instinct is to snooze away in the evenings. I loathe those weird strolls down the high street, lit only by streetlamps and the glow of shop windows, with a chill creeping up your coat sleeves. I dislike how forlorn four o'clock may feel, with the air damp and the sun's corrective energy absent. My yoga class has been cancelled, and I'm scared to go out into the night for anything as simple as a social drink. The thought of driving is terrifying—those impassable highways with unknown borders; the dance you must perform with the full beam, flipping it on and off, on and off. It is more desirable to stay at home. I do not mind staying at home. I understand that for many people, it feels like a significant constraint on their freedom, but it works brilliantly for me. Winter is a tranquil house illuminated by lamplight, a stroll around the garden to see the bright stars on a clear night, the roar of the wood-burning stove, and the aroma of burnt wood. It's the teapot warming up and preparing cups of bitter cocoa, soups fashioned from bones, and dumplings floating like clouds. It's quiet reading and watching movies in the afternoon twilight. The bundle consists of thick socks and a cardigan.

In the summer, I get six to seven hours of sleep per night, while in the winter, I get closer to nine. I start thinking about going to bed as soon as the sun goes down. My mother's side ingrained in me the habit of sleeping early; none of us are night owls, nor are we particularly early risers. We all require rest. I went through numerous phases in my reaction to this: as a child, I thought it was hilarious that my grandparents tucked themselves in at the same time as me; as a young adult, I thought it was delightfully quaint. As I grew older, my urge to sleep became increasingly bothersome, and I fantasised about having the extra time that, say, a five-hour night would bring. Being a mom changed my opinion on it. Some people thrive on sleep deprivation, but I do not. I've realised that I can achieve far more in nine hours than in the extra time provided by a short night. Sleeping provides me with peace, warmth, and an addictive feeling. I'm confident that my decision not to have a second child is directly tied to my devotion to sleep. Winter nights are the most pleasant. I prefer a thick duvet and a cool bedroom so that I can cuddle up against the cold. Unlike those horrible thrashing summer nights when the room is usually too cramped to enable that final tumble into unconsciousness, the chilly winter nights allow me to sleep deeply and have long, beautiful dreams. When I wake up in the middle of the night, the blackness appears deeper and velvetier than normal, nearly limitless. Winter is a season when I may withdraw and be quietly secluded, allowing me to unwind and feel refreshed. But my peaceful repose has been interrupted in recent weeks. The "terrible threes" are the dark insomniac hours when my mind emerges, fully charged, in the middle of the night. It always happens at three a.m.: long beyond midnight, but far too early to give up and begin the day. In the deepest night, I lie in the dark and fantasise. Tonight, I awoke from a dream in which I was hauled into a big wicker man and burned. It's a terrible fantasy, with a gothic sense of persecution that makes me laugh out loud. What a foolish little human I am, dreaming such obvious things and waking up with my heart racing and my throat constricted. Still, it keeps me from falling back asleep. This cliché has had a significant physiological influence. I'm aware of the hazard. I keep a tight watch on the pillows. I roll onto my side, plump my pillows, and sip from the bottle I keep nearby. The night is settling in. If only someone would pay me to worry, I could earn a living. What am I worried about during these sleepless nights? Death. Money. Failure. The familiar horsemen of the silent apocalypses that take place only after the sun has set. In the middle of the night, I may envision my house sitting on the edge of a cliff, about to tumble onto the rocks underneath. I am constantly one missed payment away from complete annihilation. I have too much debt. I have nothing. I have much too many possessions. The weight of all of the rubbish in the loft above will eventually force the bedroom ceiling to collapse. At this hour of the night, the central heating produces a strange noise, and I believe the pump is on its last legs. I should bring H up and have him listen to it to see if he agrees. It could be spewing carbon monoxide into our bedroom as we sleep. Whole families die this way, quietly and in the middle of the night. I can't shake the feeling that I might lose H one day due to appendicitis.

It's possible that everything is completely unexpected. And what would I do in that situation? Except for a collection of dusty books, I have nothing to show for my nearly forty years on this world. Yet here I am, getting closer to the abyss, losing the stable underpinnings of my existence by leaving my secure job. In the light of day, I can recall the stress that led to my decision to leave—the increasing intrusion into my family life. But just during the daytime, when I value things like serenity and independence. I'm experiencing a dyspeptic episode of conservatism in the dark. I should have a savings account with one year's earnings in it. I should have appropriate life insurance. I must've squandered something. I'm not sure what happened or when, but I despise myself for it. My life's precariousness has struck me hard. The teeth can be felt in my stomach. I am nothing, nobody, and have failed. The ego is like a lit match: bright, blue, and transitory. I'm thankful to be alone when this happens so that I may let it burn out peacefully. We should be grateful for the solitude of a winter night. They prevent us from revealing our ugliest sides to the rest of the world. I turn again, adjust the blankets, and sip more water. Two whiskeys, late and resolutely drunk, reveal their presence in my temples. I should have known better, but my tendency is to exacerbate the situation. I am not going to sleep right now. Attempting is pointless. My heart is beating beneath the duvet, and I'm hard to breathe. I sat on the edge of the bed, my feet frozen, looking for my slippers. I massage my eyes and look for my spectacles.

I head downstairs to look for my notebook.

Hazel Ryan sorts through the wood shavings and straw in a wooden box.

"Yes," she replies, "here she is."

She dips her hand in and pulls out a ball of yellow fur the size of the walnut. A dormouse is hibernating. It's spherical and compact, with little pink feet tucked into its tummy, ears drawn back, and a black-tipped tail wrapped around its head, as if to hold everything together. Hazel places the dormouse in my palm and rolls it around like a marble. It's lighter than air and shockingly cold, but yet soft and squishy. It could not be mistaken for dead. It is in a deep slumber, resting until summer.

In the United Kingdom, only three natural mammals hibernate: bats, hedgehogs, and dormice. On cold days, other creatures, such as frogs and badgers, go into torpor, decreasing their body temperature and slowing their breathing and heart rate in order to conserve energy for short periods. True hibernation, on the other hand, happens when this chilling and slowing continues for an extended period of time and is unaffected by ambient temperature or the immediate availability of food.

Dormice don't have a defined schedule; their hibernation is governed by the weather. They spend the early fall accumulating reserves of the liquid brown fat that makes them squishy to the touch; as Hazel shows, the layer of fat beneath a hibernating dormouse's skin is so fluid that fingerprints can be left on it. This is a readily available energy store to see them through the following lengthy months. So, starting in September, they eat hedgerow fruits like blackberries, hazelnuts, and chestnuts in an attempt to double their body weight from half an ounce to a hefty ounce and a half. They must do this quickly, at a rate of around one gram each day. They might grow obese during periods of excess. They will attempt to prolong hibernation until they are plump enough to survive in times of scarcity. They must, however, be prepared when the first frosts approach. Dormice have a high surface area to volume ratio, so they can quickly lose heat. They build their nest, a compact ball of moss, bark, and leaves, in the days leading up to hibernation. They live in trees throughout the summer, but the temperature difference is too great, therefore their hibernation nests are built in dips in the ground, maybe around tree roots. They want to create an environment that absorbs rain and dew, allowing the nest to stay damp throughout the winter. This may not sound pleasant, but it is crucial for dormice survival: they are so small that they would desiccate during their long sleep if they did not receive external moisture.

When they have found the appropriate location, they squeeze themselves tightly into their nest and close the opening. "If you can't find a door," Hazel says, "there's a dormouse in it." They generally hibernate alone, but a recent radio-tracking research found evidence of nest sharing. This could happen when there is a limited selection of habitat. Dormice will seek out the ideal climate, and if there aren't many possibilities, they may be compelled to share—sharing is more common in captivity. Dormices will lower their body temperature to match that of their surroundings, which is usually 5°C or lower, while they are safe in their hibernating nest. To properly hibernate, they need to be just above freezing. When they warm up to 6°C, their metabolic rate rises and they begin to burn fat; below zero, they must also rely on their fat reserves to avoid freezing. If they achieve the appropriate temperature, they will hibernate from October to May, slowing their metabolic rate, breathing extremely slowly, and matching the temperature of the outside world until the first days of summer, when there will be enough insects to feed on. Even when they awaken, they will fall into torpor when food is scarce, such as when it rains or during the "hungry gap" between their preferred crops. Dormice spend more time asleep than awake.

I had always imagined hibernation as a long, monotonous sleep, but Hazel informs me that dormice wake up every ten days to rest in their nests while temporarily resuming their metabolism. This, it is assumed, allows their kidneys to filter out poisons while also giving them valuable time to ensure that their nest is safe. Hazel is a senior conservation officer at the Wildwood Trust in Kent, and the dormice she cares for may be underweight as winter approaches. They frequently come from orphaned litters or litters that were mistimed for the seasons. Others have been found by chance in their nests. Because they are more likely to die during their hibernation, they are hauled from their warm beds at regular intervals to be weighed, which I am currently seeing. I'd like to say I'm helping, but I think I'm just getting in the way and cooking a lot.

It's hard to think of anything more objectively lovely than a dormouse: tiny, fluffy, and sleepy, they appear almost eager to receive human attention. They are also quite vulnerable: the hazel dormice population has been declining for some time, and they are now considered endangered. Dormice have been left behind as the world has changed. Seasons are shifting, hedgerows and woodland ecosystems are disappearing, and food sources are depleting. They may be too feeble to live in the industrialised world, but for the time being, they symbolise laziness. I began working downstairs at 4 a.m. Getting up in the middle of the night felt insane, but with a hot cup of tea in my hand, I view it as a need for normalcy. My thoughts have collected like snowflakes in a snow globe now that I'm upright.

Everything gets back into focus. I clear my desk's surface and create a pool of light with my lamp. I leave to find some matches and light a candle. One light is consistent and reliable, whereas the other is irregular and flashing. I open my notebook and start working on these two extremes. On balance, I'd rather be in the middle. Certainty is a fixed state with little potential for growth. It's painful to waver. I'm glad I'm halfway between the two. I can discover a slanting affinity for this time of night, the almost-morning, if I stop trying to fall asleep and reclaim my attention. As the only person awake, I love the opportunity to relax in privacy. It's a low-demand time in the 24-hour cycle. Nobody can reasonably expect you to check texts or emails, and social media scrolling feeds have gone silent. Finally, this represents seclusion in a world where it is difficult to feel alone. Even the cats realise it is too early to demand food. They raise an ear as I pass and then return to their coiled balls. This is a time when very few activities seem acceptable. At this hour, I mostly read, scrutinising the stack of books near my favourite chair, waiting to share snippets of wisdom rather than inviting cover-to-cover reading. I read a chapter here, a part there, or look through an index for a subject that interests me. I appreciate free-form, exploratory reading. For the first time, I'm not reading to escape; instead, having already escaped, I'm free to explore the additional space I've discovered, as restless and impatient as I want, revelling in the game of my own focus. They believe we should dance like no one is watching. That, I think, also applies to reading. The inky hours are also for writing: the scratch and flow of a pen on fine paper, the stuttering chains of words that fill pages upon pages. Writing can feel like a race against your own mind at times, as your hand fights to keep up with the flow of your thoughts, and I feel this most strongly at night, when there are no competing demands on my attention. That sleepy, confused state erodes the barriers of my waking brain. My dreams continue, adding another layer to my perspective. Most crucially, my reasonable daily self, who is demanding and dominant, is still sleeping. Without its watchful eye, I can dream up new possibilities and take innovative risks. I can confess all of my transgressions to a piece of paper without fear of being censored.

If my night-waking feels primal to me, it's because it was once a normal element of human sleep, but was recently lost. According to historian A. Roger Ekirch's book At Day's End: Night in Times, Prior to the Industrial Revolution, it was typical to split the night into two phases of sleep: the "first sleep," or "dead sleep," which lasted from the evening until the early hours of the morning, and the "second" or "morning" sleep, which safely brought the slumberer to daylight. During the "watch," which lasted an hour or more, "families rose to urinate, smoke tobacco, and even visit close neighbours." Many others made love, prayed, and... focused on their dreams, resulting in immense tranquillity and self-awareness." In the closeness of the darkness, families and lovers might engage in long, intricate, wandering conversations that would not be appropriate during the bustling daylight. This was the outcome of the days when the night was actually dark, when the poor went to bed early to save money on candles, and even the wealthy had to choose between working in low light or falling asleep. Because the streets were usually dark outside the house, the sole living area was within. Little was written about this routine, and most likely private, part of the day. Ekirch discovers brief mentions of the first and second sleeps in diaries, letters, and literature, but this ancient practice is nearly invisible to the modern eye. In 1996, Thomas Wehr and his colleagues attempted to mimic the conditions of prehistoric winter sleep by depriving people of artificial light for fourteen hours each night and seeing what happened to their sleep patterns. After a few weeks, the participants formed the practice of staying awake in bed for two hours before falling asleep for four hours. They would then wake up and spend two or three hours meditating and relaxing before sleeping for four more hours until sunrise. Wehr's most surprising observation was that his patients did not experience stress throughout the midnight watch. During these moments, they felt quiet and reflective, and blood tests revealed elevated levels of prolactin, the hormone that causes nursing mothers to produce more breast milk. Prolactin levels are normally low in both men and women, but the watch appeared to have "an endocrinology all of its own," which Wehr compared to a heightened state of awareness similar to meditation. Our forefathers may have experienced a condition of being unlike any we know, or can know, unless we reject the incursion of artificial light into this borderland between wakefulness and sleep. Maybe my insomnia isn't solely from worrying about the future. In the twenty-first century, we are surrounded by light, not just from the chandeliers and lights that purposely illuminate our houses in the evening, but also from the ever-increasing legions of electronic devices that flicker, pulse, and glow to let us know what they are doing. Nowadays, light might feel like an intruder, carrying a piece of knowledge or a responsibility with it.

Even when left alone on the sideboard, my phone is a restless creature, writhing into life to announce a new message, an update, or a reminder of something I'm attempting to forget. I've been looking for an alarm clock that lets me check the time without lighting up the room for years, but I've finally given up. The digital LED clock's green glow kept me awake; the traditional clock with luminous hands was impossible to read; and the "night glow" clock, which only lit up when I pressed a button, burned my eyeballs in the middle of the night, leaving eerie blue phantoms behind my eyelids when I tried to sleep again. Add to that my television (yes, I am one of those sinners who likes to fall asleep while watching a comedy show), with its piercing red standby light that is difficult to turn off, and the back neighbours, who feel compelled to illuminate their yard every evening. Light is unavoidable. The local council in my town is gradually replacing old orange-toned sodium lamps with newer, brighter LED lamps. The dark—and our fears that lurk in it—are being pushed further back, but residents are complaining that they can't sleep; light sneaks through blackout blinds and double-layered drapes.

We don't have enough nights remaining. We've lost touch with our natural impulses for darkness, which invites us to spend time with our dreams. Our personal winters are usually marked by insomnia: perhaps we are drawn to that specific zone of closeness and introspection, darkness and alone, without completely comprehending what we are yearning for. Perhaps we are being encouraged to seek our own comfort after all.

Sleep is not a void, but rather a gateway to a different kind of consciousness—introspective and restorative, full of tangential thoughts and unexpected revelations. In the winter, we are treated to a different type of sleep: a slow, ambulatory process in which waking thoughts merge with dreams and space is created in the darkest hours to repair the fragmented narratives of our days.

However, we are inhibiting our inherent ability to process the difficult aspects of life. My personal midnight terrors vanish when I turn insomnia into a watch: a designated sacred space when I can do nothing but contemplate. Here, I am given a position in the middle, as if I had discovered a hidden door, the stuff of fantasies. Even dormice understand how to do it: they wake up for a few minutes to take care of business before falling back asleep.

Winter continually offers us liminal spaces to dwell in, but we reject them. The frigid season's role is to teach us how to greet them.

CHAPTER 7
MIDWINTER

My phone's alarm goes off at quarter-to-five. I get out of a foreign bed and change into my clothes: a thermal vest, long johns, slacks, a T-shirt, and a sweater. Wear ski socks under your walking boots. I've already packed a winter coat, scarf, mittens, and cap in the car's trunk. I meet my friend downstairs in the kitchen, where she is making a cup of tea. We guzzled it silently, worried about the traffic. Are we leaving on time? We had better get started. We get our kids out of bed and repeat the same routine: socks, long johns, vests, jeans, and sweaters. We wrap them in blankets and tell them they can sleep in the car, even though we know they won't. We drive into Amesbury in the dead of night, the children in the back of the car becoming increasingly agitated. I was expecting more: a continual stream of pilgrims to Stonehenge, a gathering of people from all over the country, all drawn to this symbol of ancestral worship on the morning of the Winter Solstice. However, we see no more vehicles entering the property than on a typical afternoon. It's around six a.m., and it's dark outside. Still, I was hoping for something more anarchic to contrast with my bland middle-class agnosticism. I'd been to a Christmas party the night before, and every time I mentioned where we were going today, I got a frightened chuckle, a sneer, or a gasp of breath. When is the Solstice? How about the crusties? Who are these tree huggers? What about hippies? What about druids? It was clear that I was ready to do something embarrassing: mark an invisible moment in the year with the New Age cult, complete with ludicrous rituals and invented religion. "You're not one of them, are you?" one man asked. Stonehenge, the famous ring of standing stones, is thought to have been created between 4,000 and 5,000 years ago. The circle is usually made up of trilithons, which are two upright stones joined by a third to form a lintel across the top. They are part of a wider complex of Neolithic and Bronze Age constructions in the Wiltshire countryside, which also includes hundreds of burial grounds. They're an imposing presence in the environment, standing four metres tall, and it's clear they had religious significance, though the specifics of that ceremony and belief have been lost over time.

Geoffrey of Monmouth stated in his Historia Regum Britanniae in the 12th century that the stones had healing properties and were brought to the site by King Aurelius Ambrosius to commemorate a war against the Saxons. He thought that Stonehenge was erected in Ireland by a race of giants, and he saw that fifteen thousand knights could not move the stones, but Merlin could due to his exceptional understanding. In the early eighteenth century, antiquarian William Stukeley investigated the surrounding earthworks and concluded that Stonehenge was a Druidic devotional site. He envisioned the ceremonies that took place there using limited historical sources, primarily Roman, that depicted Druids as magical savages, both fundamentally different and powerless in the face of an organised military force. Stukeley appears to have made up as much as he revealed, but he developed a fascination with the location and came to identify as a Druid, adopting the Druidic name Chyndonax. Stonehenge became a famous tourist site for Victorians, who travelled in large numbers to see the dawn at midsummer. Tourists were given chisels and encouraged to remove their own personal presents from the monument at the time. Despite multiple academic debunkings of the Druidic connection, the association has survived, and in the twentieth century, Stonehenge became increasingly important to modern-day Druids and other pagan groups, at a time when society as a whole strove to safeguard and preserve its legacy. This has frequently caused disputes. Access to the stones was initially restricted in 1978 owing to worries about erosion as tourist numbers surged. After the site was closed to those planning to attend the annual midsummer Stonehenge Free Festival in 1985, there was a violent clash between New Age pilgrims and police. The "exclusion zone" around the stones remained in place until 1999, when activists obtained a ruling from the European Court of Human Rights that confirmed Stonehenge as a place of worship and asserted the right of several groups to worship there, including spiritualists, pagans, and Druids. When the moratorium was lifted, English Heritage recommended that solstice celebrations be peaceful and polite, and no incidents have been reported since. Aside from their ancient origins, the stones are significant because of their astrological alignment. Every year around midsummer, the longest day begins with the sun rising behind the Heel Stone and shining directly into the centre of the circle. The shortest day of the year once ended with the sun setting between the two upright stones of the circle's tallest trilithon. Because this structure no longer exists, the celebration is now held the next morning, honouring the sunrise as the days finally begin to lengthen. This is what we've come to expect: the spectacle of light returning and the happiness that comes with it. I'm not sure what I anticipated to see here in midwinter, but the reality is a lot more pleasant. We stand in line behind happy men and women in their late forties, the majority of whom look to have just exited Mountain Warehouse, but some are clothed in cloaks. One man put on a Green Man mask and covered his face with a mound of nylon oak leaves. The atmosphere is polite and relaxing. The café has nettle wine and mead in its fridges, but no one seems to be drinking. We may be lining up at the Women's Institute tent at the village fete. I order sausage buns and hot chocolate for the kids, and we sit outside in the unusually warm night, discussing when we should visit the henge. As their patience runs out, we board a shuttle bus labelled "To the Stones," and our fellow passengers make a nice grandparental fuss over the children. Then we're free to see Stonehenge for the first time, as the sky clears to a midnight blue before sunrise. A throng has gathered around the stones, and they are not of the English Heritage gift-shop variety; rather, it feels like the conclusion of a rock festival, replete with the necessary good-natured police officers and first-aiders on hand to treat drug casualties. When I ask one of them if she expects a lot of business, she says the winter solstice is quiet, but all-night celebrations are more usual in the summer. There are people dressed in ponchos and capes, dreadlocked New Age pilgrims, women dressed in long mediaeval gowns, and a man clad in a silver space suit playing a melodica. Music can be heard all around, including several drums, a singing bowl, and a few squeezebox chords. People either dance or stand and watch. A hobbyhorse, someone dressed in concentric circles and wrapped in multicoloured rags, is buffeting us. It's a disorienting mix of cultures, and I feel out of place among them, if only because I lack their enthusiasm. There are a few families who look a lot like us, a little uncomfortable in our dowdy outdoor gear and unsure how or not to engage in the festivities. Our first inclination is to admonish the children for getting too close to the stones, rather than inviting them to commune with them. We are intruders, although I am not sure what that means in this context. There is no way we are not welcome, and the crowd is too diverse for us to really stand out. If merely wanting to spend the solstice beside the stones is sufficient reason, we are not intruders. I really don't know how to worship in this manner.

The goal here is euphoria, but not the kind that the first-aiders are seeking. Some seek it via dancing and song, while others stand quietly, eyes closed, touching the stones. The chance to get up close to the trilithons, touch them, and genuinely feel their height and mass is an incredible luxury that can be had for the little cost of an early morning. When I've seen them before, from the protection of the tourist trail, they've always appeared little, uniform, and underwhelming to me. They are no longer any of these things; they are green and yellow, covered in lichens and filled with crevices and protrusions. You can imagine them being excavated from a quarry, shaped, moved over land, and carefully positioned by human hands. It's great to be here, smelling their damp scent and gaining an understanding of their organisation. I weave between them, heading for the inner circle, which is becoming increasingly packed with red-clad people. Something is about to happen, and you can feel the anticipation growing. My watch says I have ten minutes before sunlight. The drumming has intensified, and smoke is coming from somewhere. We gathered the children, and I lifted Bert onto my shoulders to look about. The density of the bodies has grown. We can no longer get closer than the outside sarsen stones, and there is singing in the centre. I can almost hear the harmonies, but not the lyrics. Nonetheless, it's compelling. I'm standing on the edge of a temple rather than an archaeological site, yet the atmosphere is chaotic and slightly heightened. The drumming becomes increasingly intense and rapid, with feverish hands groping for a beat and sentences yelled with greater vigour. I can't see very well, and I doubt anyone else can. There's no order of service or hymn sheet, and there's no sense that we're all expected to be thinking the same thing or even coming for the same reason. The gorgeous mishmash has left me slightly perplexed but mostly happy.

The murky pre-dawn lightens to blinding white at some undetermined moment as the sun rises, albeit invisibly behind a bank of clouds. People from all tribes join hands and hug, exclaiming, "We have turned the year!" We do it as well, much to the dismay of the children, who have grown absorbed in a fantasy in which the stones are dragons and they are their caregivers. There is no single point of release. It's similar to a failed orgasm—the lengthy, slow, breath-holding buildup that results in nothing. The meaning remains the same either way. Following months of approaching darkness, light has returned to the globe. I stay near the circle for a long time after that, hoping the clouds will clear so I can see the golden ball framed by standing stones. But this is not to be. We return to the visitor centre by going around the nearby barrows. There is a classic view of situations like this: good old English eccentrics, a touch goofy and dumb, but ultimately harmless. We don't like large celebrations unless they involve football. We are sceptical of clothes and the desire for ritual. We like to temper our religion with an apologetic tone and a sense of humility. Sermons must bore us. Prayers should be spoken quietly. Singing must be done as a gloomy need, in the quietest voice possible, by people with firm personal boundaries. It is unrelated to the pursuit of ecstasy.

The following day, I review the news coverage to determine what I should have made of it all. Photographs of strange, wild-looking people in eccentric clothes hugging stones can be found in a few newspapers. The BBC focuses on a parking conflict that I was absolutely unaware about. According to the Daily Star, we all "descended" on Stonehenge, as if we were a massive invasion force from above. AccuWeather described the unseen sunrise as "spectacular." It's tough not to believe that all of the content was created ahead of time and distributed online without much thought, existing solely to gratify readers who will tut and shake their heads at these weirdos' idiocy. There are already videos available. The YouTube comments section is a mix of condescension and hellfire-and-brimstone preaching, with a dash of racism thrown in: "THIS IS PURE SATANIC!" yells one; "heathens," screams another; and "these are hippies, don't compare it to our slavic ancestors," exclaims a third. "Fake pagans" ; "bunch of crack heads" ; "I smell marijuana." (I didn't.)

What I saw at Stonehenge did not offend me in any way. Maybe part of it wasn't to my liking, and some of it made me wonder what the connection was between the location, the belief, and the action. But none of this was my issue, and no one bothered to question why I was there. It was obviously a jumble of different spiritualities, yet it struck me as incredibly tolerant. Here was a group of folks ready to share their preferred place of worship while also respecting one another's styles of celebration. They did not seek the oppressive voice of consistency or uniformity, nor did they blame one another for choosing a different route. They simply did their thing and let others do theirs.

I'm becoming increasingly drawn to moments like this: a respite from the year's monotonous march and a way to mark the transition to the next phase. But that desire makes me squirm, like if it's a perversion I'm ashamed to admit in public. Rituals have always struck me as somewhat ridiculous. It feels strange to need—to want—this one. After reading a piece in The Times in which he admits to experiencing the same twitching sensation, I contacted Philip Carr-Gomm, the leader of the Order of Bards, Ovates, and Druids. "I think Druidry is a bit wacky myself," he says, "but then, a lot of what's going on in the world is wacky." Trump is unusual. "I find Anglican bishops in their robes strange."The biggest dread of the English, as John Cleese once observed, is embarrassment, and I am saddled with it."

I, too, am troubled by the notion that, rather than being immoral, hurtful, or stupid, inventing rituals to discover more purpose in the world is merely cringeworthy. When I screw up my nose when explaining the Stonehenge solstice, Philip laughs kindly. He quit attending church a few years ago. He still observes the solstice in a more modest fashion, but he sees it as part of a series of celebrations that occur at regular intervals to make life more pleasant.

"Druids follow the eightfold Wheel of the Year," he goes on to say, "so we have something to do every six weeks." It is an important period of time since you can always glimpse what will happen in the future. "It establishes a trend throughout the year."

According to his book Druid Mysteries, the winter solstice marks the beginning of the new year. Druids practise a ritual in which they "cast away whatever impedes the appearance of light" and throw scraps of fabric on the ground in the dark to represent the things that have kept them back. Then, using a flint, a lone lamp is lit and hoisted in the east to usher in a new cycle, culminating at the summer solstice. The next festival is Imbolc on February 1st, when the first snowdrops bloom, their little white blooms shivering in the cold. It represents the end of winter, when snow would ordinarily melt and rubbish could be cleared away, but it also marks the beginning of spring, when the first lambs are born. The spring equinox, when the days and nights are the same length, will soon arrive, and Alban Eilir (the Light of the Earth) will be commemorated. Beltane is observed on May Day, when spring is in full bloom and cattle are usually liberated from their winter captivity. This arrangement continues throughout the summer until we reach Samhain, the end of the year and the start of the final time before being restored at the winter solstice. Four solar festivals, associated with solstices and equinoxes, and four pastoral festivals in between, remembering significant events in the year's lived experience.

"In mainstream culture, the only major festival is now Christmas," says Philip, "and possibly a summer vacation." The chasm is just too huge. When you follow a path like Druidism, the pattern of festivals gives a rhythm, allowing you to navigate through even the darkest periods."

Is this a made-up religion that combines borrowed traditions and refers to a fake past when mysticism reigned supreme? Probably. Maybe. But it does not appear to matter to me. It expresses a yearning that many of us may connect to. Have we really advanced so far in the realm of electric light and central heating that the rhythm of the year has become irrelevant to us, and we no longer care when the hours begin to shorten again? If our current society is unable to offer us with the meanings we seek, it is perfectly acceptable to reconsider or create other methods of doing so. "Do you pray?" author Jay Griffiths wonders in her 2019 Aeon magazine essay "Daily Grace". "Yes, I pray," she murmurs to herself, "earthwise rather than to any off-ground god—and, though I cannot tell you the words I use, I will tell you their core is beauty."

I'm embarrassed to admit this, but I pray on Earth as well. I started meditating over a decade ago, and when children made it difficult to sit for twenty minutes twice a day, I found a way to distil some of that experience. I can achieve some of the serenity that meditation brings by closing my eyes, even if just for a second, and focusing my attention on the centre of my perception. I've come to think of it as prayer, even though I don't ask for anything or speak to anyone. It's a strong nonverbal sense, like a brief breath of pure existence in the midst of a forest of words. It is an untangling, a chance to feel the real ache of wanting, the soothing wash of self-compassion, the heart swell of appreciation, and the tick tick tick of being. I feel most connected to others when I am alone. In a crowd, I can feel entirely isolated, yet when I close my eyes, it's as if I've stepped into a river of all consciousness, saturated with common humanity.

I hesitate to write these lines since I don't have friends who pray or discuss the world in this way. I'm ashamed of this. I'm seeking for simple vocabulary to describe what I'm saying. I avoid religious certainty and the intentionally noncommittal terminology I see online—the internet-spiritual, which celebrates the moments in which we are blessed and grateful but is cautious to identify the source of our blessing or thanks. In the spirit of many twelve-step programs, I couldn't defer to a higher power unless I knew exactly who that higher power was, what they wanted me to believe, and whether I shared their ideals. I am a very sensible person who is prone to inquiring. I cannot stand uncertainty. I require a methodical understanding of any beliefs I may hold. I require that they make logical sense.

But, as worldly as my prayers are, they transport me to a location I can't dissect or examine, a territory beyond language. When I'm not praying, it's difficult for me to imagine a deity to whom I'd want to pray. Still, I'm drawn to prayer for the sake of prayer. My mind knows the act, and it occurs without my assistance. Carol Ann Duffy's best-known poem, "Prayer," begins, "Some days, although we cannot pray, a prayer / utters itself." I pray because it is something that I am capable of doing. It appears that I have an atavistic inclination, a need to find life in the world around me, in the trees, stones, and pools of water, as well as the birds and critters that cross my path. My conscious brain keeps my personal animism quiet, while my unconscious cultivates it. A prayer, on the other hand, is something done silently and privately. There's nothing to market or debate, so I can be discreet about it, appearing to be rationalists while secretly seeking the numinous. This urge for ritual is unique and frightening since it exposes my hidden devotions. But I found enormous comfort in sitting in the Swedish church and listening to the choir, and I felt a definite boost from joining the crowd at Stonehenge and being a part of the effort to remember the end of one year and the beginning of the next. Since visiting the Stonehenge solstice, I've noticed something new: the sun rises a little earlier every morning, making it easier to get out of bed. Celebrating that transformation in front of others had an impact. It added a little joy to the simple act of noticing and strengthened the dark need lying behind it with fellow human souls. It reduced some of the shame associated with requiring it. The free communities seen in spiritual or religious gatherings were once completely normal to us, but joining them now appears more radical, a bold challenge to the nuclear family's strictures, the desire to keep within small friendship groups, and the avoidance of the awe-inspiring. Congregations are adaptable, accommodating a diverse spectrum of people while producing unexpected perspectives and discoveries. "We need them now more than ever before."Griffiths describes rituals as "psyche doorways" that connect the holy and profane, purity and dirt, beauty and ugliness, and an entryway from the ordinary into the extraordinary. For my part, they provide a forum for feelings that I would otherwise dismiss as silly or ridiculous: a mute amazement at the passage of time. Everything is changing. Everything remains the same. Those things are bigger than me and more than I can take.

Winter, more than any other season, needs a metronome to time its hardest beats and provide us with a tune to follow into spring. The year will continue anyway, but by paying attention to it, feeling its beat, and watching transitions—perhaps even taking the time to think about what we want from the next phase of the year—we can gain a sense of it.

CHAPTER 8
EPIPHANY

When you start paying attention to winter, you realise that we have a thousand winters in our lives, some big and others small. Just as I thought I was nearing the end of H's and my sicknesses, and that life was about to resume again, I discovered that a glorious winter had arrived without my knowing. My child was too afraid to attend school. At six years old, Bert was already overwhelmed by the poisonous soup of thirty kids jammed into one classroom, a teacher pulled in so many different directions that he felt invisible, and a few vicious guys on the playground. A fast-paced curriculum that made him feel like he couldn't keep up; a set of broad goals that meant "expected" was all we ever heard about him. I was aware of his fears since I had been paying attention. But I hadn't really listened. The gravity of the situation took me off guard. I imagined his troubles were common, but they were not. I'd offered calming words, a few tiny attempts at problem solving, and the reassurance that the best people dislike school. A commotion was precisely what he needed. He asked me to step up and say, "You know what? This is insufficient. "My son is entitled to happiness!"

Because he was not satisfied. I hadn't seen the delight leaking from him, but it had. Some winters are more gentle than others. Some winters creep up on us so slowly that they infiltrate every area of our life before we realise. His outburst at school appeared surprising, but it was not. He had been telling me about it all along, and now he was double-checking to make sure I had heard correctly. So I finally gave his words some thought. I yanked him out of school and ignored suggestions on how to reintroduce him: scare and cajole him; charm him into enduring it; or drug him into obedience. I would never do those things. I wasn't willing to break him just to get him back in school, no matter how desperate I was for my own time. I, who had previously enjoyed the rhythm and challenge of school, realised how many others saw school as an absolute endurance—yet many of them believed that our children, too, should endure it for fourteen wretched years of their life. I was supposed to be more concerned about his future qualities than his ability to be fulfilled. That wasn't something I was willing to do. I didn't feel that fulfilling your potential and not being completely miserable were mutually exclusive. Happiness is the most important skill we can ever develop. It is not a part of ourselves that deserves to be banished to the shameful realm of the intentionally naive. Happiness is our potential, the outcome of allowing our minds to think as they should, having enough of what they require, and being free of the crushing weight of bullying and humiliation. We tolerate working conditions as children that we would find intolerable as adults: constant exposure of our accomplishment to a hostile audience; motivation by threat rather than encouragement (and big threats, too: if you don't do this, you'll ruin your entire future life...); and the social world in which you're mocked and teased, your most embarrassing desires exposed, and your newly formed body subjected to the kind of scrutiny that would destroy an adult. This is sometimes accompanied by physical threats throughout childhood, such as being pushed and shoved on the playground, punched, and kicked. On your way home, there's always the possibility of something worse hiding around the corner. Consider how it would feel to be an adult facing a constant threat to your bodily and mental health. We would never accept it now, but we did as children because it was expected of us and we didn't know any better. However, if happiness is a skill, so is sadness. Perhaps all those years at school, or other terrors, trained us to ignore sadness, stuffing it down our satchels and pretending it doesn't exist. We frequently have to learn as adults to hear the clarity of its appeal. That's how winter looks. It actively accepts sadness. Allowing oneself to experience it as a necessity is the discipline. It takes courage to confront the most negative aspects of our existence and commit to repairing them as best we can. Winter is a period of intuition, when we may feel our inner needs as clearly as a knife.

It was time to teach my son about winter. It is a difficult skill to teach. So we took our time and engaged in activities that we enjoyed, such as playing on the beach and exploring the library. We made pirates out of air-drying clay and went for a walk in the woods to gather pine cones and berries. We took the train to London and visited the Natural History Museum to observe the dinosaurs in peace. We used hoarfrost on an abnormally cold morning to create oddly impenetrable snowballs. We baked cookies, kneaded pizza dough, and played Minecraft more than I'd like. We went through some difficult things together. I will not pretend that it was pleasurable. Regardless, it was essential. We screamed and cried together. We were paralysed by fear. We worried, slept it off, didn't sleep, and allowed our schedules to fall apart. We did not flee the world, but rather allowed it to retreat from us. We howled in anguish to our friends and family, and we were surprised by how many people came in to aid us, sometimes with actual assistance, sometimes simply by sharing their own experiences. It was beneficial. We were broken into pieces, yet we had never felt more loved.

During the winter, we experienced a change. We read, worked, brainstormed, and came up with new solutions. We switched our focus from maintaining a normal life to constructing a new one. When everything is broken, it is available for purchase. That is winter's gift: it is tempting. Whether we like it or not, change is inevitable. We can leave with a different coat. The finest counsel came from individuals who had already been through this winter. I first met them on a Wednesday morning while sitting at a boisterous trampoline park, feeling conspicuously like I was accompanying a school-age child. I was expecting a tap on the shoulder, either from the centre management or a lurking truancy cop, assuming they still exist. However, the tap on the shoulder came from a woman at an adjacent table who was part of a group. "Are you a homeschooler, too?" she said.

And I blurted out what appeared to be my entire life history, or at least everything that had gone wrong in the previous months. My story was met with smiles and nods, sympathetic tilts of the head, rather than fury at my failure as a mother. "I'd say everyone around this table has been through exactly the same thing," she said to me.

I could have cried right there, just knowing I wasn't alone. I sat down with them and realised that my child was one of hundreds of children throughout the country who felt crushed by school, and that I was one of hundreds of parents who had a deep reluctance to force their children back into it and train them to accept the consequences. The parents told me that it took some time, but their children found happiness outside of traditional schools after being violently unhappy in it. "She's a different child now," one of them explained. "She's recovered a part of herself that we thought was lost forever." I followed her eyes to a little girl who was whirling and skipping between the trampolines, a vision of freedom. And my own child, who was happily playing with another boy in the group.

"Take a look at these. "They're like two peas in a pod," she explained. I felt accepted in a way I hadn't experienced in months.

Another truth of wintering is that you will learn wisdom during your time there, and it is your responsibility to pass it on thereafter. It is our responsibility to listen to those who have wintered before us. It's a gift transaction in which nobody loses. This may mean breaking a lifelong habit that has been carefully passed down through generations: viewing other people's catastrophes and feeling that they brought it on themselves in ways that you would never do. This is not only a terrible attitude. It damages us because it hinders us from learning about disasters and how to prepare for them. It hinders us from reaching out to others in need. And when our own misfortune occurs, we are forced into a humiliating retreat as we try to find errors we never committed or wrongheaded attitudes we never had in the beginning. Either that, or we become convinced that there is someone else to blame. We learn from watching winter and truly listening to its teachings that the result is sometimes disproportionate to the cause; that minor errors can lead to catastrophic consequences; and that life is frequently dreadfully unjust, but it continues regardless of our agreement. We become more empathetic to other people's troubles as they frequently presage our own. I allowed Bert to stay up late one night to finish watching the final Harry Potter film. We'd begun reading the novels at the start of his issues, and it was clear that he was identified with Harry: tormented and belittled, prone to outbreaks of wrath, but also brave and devoted, a boy who toughs it out in the bad times and appreciates the good. We promptly switched to movies so he could finish them faster. He'd reached the end of Deathly Hallows: Part 1 and was so depressed that I had to show him how everything ended, that the tide would turn. As the film begins, I take out a pencil and a piece of paper and sketch the identical graphic I used to show my undergraduate students: a curve on a graph that resembles a lopsided smile.

"This is the shape of a good story," I'm going to remark. "This is the beginning and the end." And, as you can see, the lowest position is always in the middle. It's known as the nadir—the point at which things have become so awful that you can't see a way out."

Bert looks at it for a while. "So that's where we are," he says, pointing to the curve's absolute bottom. "Here."

I'm not sure if we're talking about our curve or Harry's. "Yes," I answer, shifting my pencil slightly to the right. "And the fightback begins here."

"So after that it all gets better?"

"No, not quite. There will be ups and downs. But, from now on, the story's hero is working on a solution. Even with each setback, he makes progress."

Bert scribbles over my line with his pencil. He stays on the initial curve, but takes several deep dives along the way.

"So this is what it's really like," he said. "This is how stories work."

"Yes," I responded. "Except that it continues to happen in real life."
"The adventure does not end with the final page."

This year, among the twelve days that I usually aim to fill meaningfully, I started a new Christmas custom. It begins at the solstice and ends on New Year's Day. I gather with a few friends at sunset after the solstice to start a fire on the beach, transporting my fire bowl and a bag of wood through town in my old shopping trolley. It's unseasonably warm, to the point where the cat moults the next morning, as if she's had enough of winter and wants to move on. Despite this, the wind whips and blasts as I try to light the newspaper beneath my kindling, blowing out fifteen matches and leaving me cursing under my breath. When someone arrives with a lighter and makes my Girl Guide attempts appear primitive, I'm beginning to suspect we won't have a fire at all. It quickly burns palely in the low, slanting light, prolonging our shadows as we stand on the rocks in our coats, clutching flasks of tea and mulled wine and drinking beer from bottles. The tide is far out. Our children run along the beach, planning which toys they will receive and challenging one another to believe in Father Christmas for another year. We stare at the sun, which is shining a golden light beneath scattered grey clouds as it approaches the horizon. Whitstable Beach is an excellent place to observe sunsets, and I enjoy soaking in a variety of them throughout the year. On certain days, it sinks into the sea to the right of the Isle of Sheppey. It has now moved to the left, behind the modest dwellings at Seasalter, and has reached its full winter extent. I've known for a long time that the sun moves across the sky during the year, but I'd never seen it before. In the winter, it provides an entirely different escape, rising over marshes rather than the sea. We see the last peak of its circle dissipate, and the fire appears to burn more intensely. I wish we could sing a song, carol, or hymn to celebrate the return of light. "We have turned the year," I add, recalling what I discovered at Stonehenge a few hours earlier. The sentence echoes across our group: we have turned the year.

The year has passed.

The year has passed.

It would have happened otherwise, with or without our knowledge, but doing it this way offers us the fleeting sense that we have gained control—not of the seasons, but of our reactions to them. The sky is now a narrow blue, visible but crisper and colder. The children rush out to find the sea's edge, only to return covered in muck and fatigued from being out in the dark. Someone brings the kids home to watch Elf, and we adults find ourselves in a relaxed state, each with our own notions. We supply fuel for the fire. A full moon rises above the town, as if from nowhere to continue where the sun left off. It soon shines clearly against the darker sky. Except for us, the beach is empty. We move closer to the fire, enjoying the silence while burning the last logs. When I lived in a house overlooking the ocean, I saw people build gigantic bonfires that burned high into the air. My little metal bowl is significantly less ambitious, yet it generates a significant amount of heat. We hope that the following year is easier. The phrase is repeated. We are almost at the conclusion of the year. At some moment, the sea begins to speak from deep inside the darkness, and we realise that the tide has turned. I am reminded once more of the calming value of ritual in my life, as well as D. H. Lawrence's words: "We must return to relation: vivid and nourishing relation to the cosmos and the universe... We must reenact the dawn, noon, and sunset rituals, as well as the rituals of starting a fire and pouring water, and taking our first and last breaths."

After failing to persuade everyone to return to the beach to see the sun rise, I stood alone in the garden the next morning. I have no clear view of the horizon, so all I can do is get my mug of tea and watch the day unfold. The stars are visible at first, brilliant specks against a dark sky. However, the birds start to move in expectation of the rising sun. The herring gulls' calls become louder, and I observe their silhouettes above me, suggesting that the stars have disappeared. When the sky is almost blue, the robin sings. Then, in the area between two houses, golden light appears, and everything returns to normal.

For me, that day marks the beginning of the Christmas season. I've left things late, as befits the end of a crisis-prone year, but I spend the morning at the local grocer, bringing in the Christmas supplies: Stilton, ham, Brussels sprouts, and an enormous capon. Unfathomable quantities of potatoes. Red and white wines, as well as a bottle of Marsala. Chocolates containing Turkish delight and cherry liqueur. A bag of satsumas, some of them wrapped in blue and gold paper. Several cream pots, just in case.

I also complete all of my holiday shopping in one go. It's a binge, a happy heaping of boxes and bundles into my cart, a dizzying handover of cash at the checkout, and it feels more philanthropic than a steady accumulation of gifts over several months. I buy Bert a new set of pyjamas every Christmas Eve, as I have since he was a baby—this year's are pale blue with bicycles. I return home feeling prepared, not as if I resisted Christmas until the last minute. Instead, I handled it in the proper context and at the appropriate time, making it enjoyable rather than a chore.

We are required to prepare a smorgasbord for Santa on Christmas Eve. Bert has prepared a lengthy list of refreshments for the great man (all of which must be labelled), as well as extra provisions for his reindeer. After that, we placed Bert's stocking on the doorknob, only to learn at the last minute that he had booby-trapped it with a looped belt in the hopes of waking up and seeing Santa. I'm sneakily pleased with his ingenuity, but less so later, when I'm trying to unravel the thing after a few glasses of Marsala. But racing downstairs to stuff a Christmas stocking is one of my year's pleasures, demonstrating kindness and attention. I like to include the usual items (gold coins and a chocolate orange in the toe for my fruit-refuser) as well as a collection of knick-knacks that are insignificant in and of themselves, but are remarkable for the intimacy they represent, the understanding of the goofy little things that will make your child smile. If Saint Nick hadn't added so much charm, I'd be tempted to detest him for taking all the credit.

On Christmas Day, we handle an avalanche of Legos, eat and drink, and play ball on the beach. On Boxing Day, we cook bubbles and squeaks and serve leftovers and pickles to our closest friends. Then comes that strange period between Christmas and New Year's, when time appears to jumble and we keep asking ourselves, "What day is it?" What is the date? I always aim to work or write on these days, but this year, like every other, I am unable to gather the necessary motivation. I used to think these were wasted days, but now I see that's exactly the point. I'm not doing anything, nor am I actively on vacation. I empty my cupboards in preparation for another year of cooking and eating. I take Bert to play with his friends. I go for cold hikes that hurt my ears. I am not sluggish. I am not being lazy. I'm simply moving my concentration for a short time away from my immediate goals for the remainder of the year. It's like I'm revving my engines.

CHAPTER 9
CHALLENGE

I've only crossed the Arctic Circle once. I was five months pregnant, anaemic, sluggish due to high blood pressure, and miserable. It wasn't the greatest idea I'd ever had, but I'd planned the vacation far in advance, before I even imagined being pregnant. Motherhood arrived sooner than I had expected. As I entered my mid-thirties, I was scared by a series of magazine pieces warning me that I was almost certainly jeopardising my future fertility, but I was also captivated by the concept that I wanted to improve my adult skills before having a kid. I felt, like I did for most of my life, that I was on the verge of having everything together and only needed a little more time. My strategy was typical of me: I decided to freeze some of my eggs till some uncertain future time when I would have figured it all out. On a rainy day that left me drenched to my underpants, I went to a fertility clinic near London Bridge for a battery of tests designed to provide an accurate picture of my viability. I was hoping to participate in a program that would allow me to gather and freeze my eggs for free in exchange for donating some of the extra ones that were hanging around unused. However, the results did not meet my expectations. The tests did not inform me how much time I had left, but rather that I did not have any. I had plenty of eggs, but I wasn't producing the essential hormones for conception. I was deluding myself into thinking I had control over the issue. I limped home that night, sending out a barrage of cheerful texts about how glad I was to have discovered this, and how information is the best armour, and I could now make informed decisions; how fortunate I was to know, in a way that so many women never do; and how I now regret all those years of experimenting with contraception. If only I had known sooner! It's very amusing. When you think about it. I then crawled into bed, pulled the covers over my head, and sobbed.

Until that point, I'd enjoyed the luxury of ambivalence, believing that depending on how my life went, I might be able to have a child or not. In any situation, I could see myself having a nice life. But suddenly it struck me like a sledgehammer: I needed a child. I'd always wanted to have a child. I hadn't had the bravery to admit it until then. Within a week, I was admitted to a different type of reproductive facility: a National Health Service IVF clinic. Our life changed dramatically in the four months before the first appointment. I had read every book I could get my hands on, bought a massive bag of ovulation detectors on eBay, and was now urinating on a stick every morning, analysing my cervical mucus, and keeping a temperature spreadsheet. We were having the kind of conception sex that quickly gets exhausting. All of this seemed really improbable to work, but I felt like I was making a difference. I was also planning to see an acupuncturist in case it could assist. My long-held antipathy to alternative treatments has evaporated. I was throwing all I owned at the problem. I'll never know what caused it, but I got pregnant at my first IVF appointment. They hurried me in for a scan, and I saw a small, writhing clump of cells with a developing heart that was still beating. It was completely unexpected and came years sooner than I'd planned, and I was terrified but desperate to cling on to this strange form of life inside me. I considered cancelling my trip to Troms because I had been ill for the entire first trimester and couldn't face the possibility. I persuaded myself it would happen during the beautiful second trimester, when everyone said I was invincible. That moment never came. In reality, I seemed to accumulate more little troubles and hurdles. But I couldn't take my mind off the possibility of heading north. In actuality, it became the standard by which I compared the gloomy, confined weeks. I almost relied on the concept to get me through. As the date arrived, my midwife expressed misgivings about whether I should go. I don't enjoy asking for permission, but in this case, I needed her to sign a document confirming that I was okay to attend, otherwise my insurance would be invalidated. I was also frightened that the airline would refuse to transport me because I was already the size of a whale and may be mistaken for a full-term Jonah. The letter, I reasoned, would save me from becoming stuck in an airport. She hesitated to make her final decision so soon, so I had to wait. I told her she had no choice but to let me go; I couldn't resist the opportunity to view the northern lights. She stared at me as if there was some new symptom to be concerned about, and she made it apparent that she was delaying for my benefit. But I think she understood as well. I felt a shift in the air, and that was the end of my adult independence. She eventually agreed four days before our trip, provided that there was appropriate emergency preparedness in place. I showed her the distance between our hotel and the hospital and told her that if necessary, I could sit and watch TV all day. Unfortunately, it was agreed that, in the worst-case scenario, the Norwegians could be relied on for maternal care.

The Arctic seemed an unusual choice for a final hurrah. We left in late January, when everything was utterly frozen and dreary. I attempted to find a warm article of clothing that would also fit over my baby tummy, and I quickly discovered the harsh biological systems that prioritised blood supply to my uterus when the temperature fell below zero, leaving me chilly. The food was excessively salty for me, and canned pineapple, my single pregnancy requirement, was rare. Because Norwegian prices were already high, we mostly ate at our accommodations, making due with pasta and the little fresh vegetables we could find. We visited the local Burger King, which brazenly claimed to be the northernmost example of its kind. But, given my blood pressure, I felt guilty. Tromso seemed more like a civilization's last outpost than the "Paris of the North." It was exactly what I needed. Polar night occurs in the Troms from the end of November until the middle of January, during which time the sun does not rise. Because the earth's axis is inclined, this region of the earth is always facing away from the sun for around forty days of the year. This does not mean that it is completely dark; rather, there is a brief moment during the day when the light is a shade of navy blue, akin to the first minutes after sunset. This may not seem like much, but to those that live it, it is the difference between day and night. Because the surrounding mountains block any view of the rising sun for an extra week, polar night lasts a little longer in Troms than it would otherwise. The sun had only just appeared when we arrived, and it was fleeting. The night seemed to last from three in the afternoon until nine in the morning. Then there was a long period of morning, with only a few days in between, before evening arrived. I wasn't there long enough to adjust, so I spent the majority of my days dozing, lulled by the monotonous midwinter drab. Sleeping in all that darkness was simple, and it provided a nice respite from the constant exhaustion. When I was awake, I was more worried about slipping on the ice, puking in public, or wandering too far from the University Hospital of North Norway, which had become my lighthouse. Winter activities were obviously out of the question, and no tour operator would let me near huskies, which were apparently known for roughhousing. I was concerned that I had been brave in all the wrong ways: that I had overreached, overcompensated for my fears, and that this would mark the end of my independence. However, there was wonder all around. Extraordinary ice escarpments line the roadsides, with babies sleeping in prams piled high with comforters, like the pea in the princess' bed. My regrets evaporated each night as we searched for the aurora borealis, the legendary northern lights, which were at their cyclical high. On the first evening, we boarded a fishing boat that travels out of Troms harbour and fed us a feast of freshly caught cod in the comfy cabin, while everyone else discussed their husky sledding injuries. We had hardly finished our meal when the skipper beckoned us to the deck, believing he had seen something, and as we stood there waiting, a wisp of greenish smoke rose overhead, almost close enough to touch. Untrained, I would have assumed it was a stray emission from one of the neighbouring boats, but it turned out to be the aurora: dim, evanescent, and tactile in ways I had not anticipated. It wasn't an image flashing across the sky, but a three-dimensional object moving slowly over our boat.

At that point, I realised that every depiction I had seen of the lights had been misleading. I'd been looking at photographs of neon displays as garish as disco lights and watching YouTube videos of lights that stood out against the night sky, bright and clear. These are typically sped up, with long exposures emphasising the vibrant greens and pinks. Every shot shows stars blazing through the aurora; the northern lights aren't bright enough to obscure little pinpoints of light from trillions of miles away. They move slowly, much like clouds in the wind. Seeing them is a risky experience, almost like a leap of faith. You had to seek for them, and I honestly don't think I would have noticed them unless I had been told they were there.

The Northern Lights are neither flashy nor demanding. They initially hide from you before whispering to you. "Is that them up there?" we'd wonder, staring at the sky. What are your thoughts? How about over there? Yes. Yes! Maybe. "I'm not sure..." But then, at a moment chosen entirely by the firmament, we were granted the gift of seeing them as a reward for our faith and patience. Then they arrived everywhere. I must have seen hundreds of movies and read dozens of papers about aurorae by now, yet I still believe I am on the cusp of understanding what they are. They are the result of a collision of forces that I was not aware of prior to organising my journey to Troms. The earth has a magnetic field, and solar winds transport charged particles—protons and electrons—from the magnetospheric plasma that surrounds us into the upper atmosphere. They ionise here, producing light and colour. I believe I understand the process as I write it down, but I know from experience that as soon as I step away from my laptop, I forget everything. The display is influenced by the particles' speed and acceleration, the latitude at which the collisions occur, and the existence of other elements—red, green, yellow, and blue are all possible, with green being the most common. The aurora borealis is most visible against a dark sky and in areas with minimal light pollution. I might have left after that first night, satisfied that I had seen all I had travelled all this way to see, but I had a sense there was more to come. So, on the second night, at ten p.m., we boarded the coach and drove for miles down roads with frozen banks on either side. Our tour guides twitched constantly on their phones to stay up to date on the newest sightings, while the coach driver performed a dangerous U-turn and sped off in a different direction several times to pursue a tipoff. Every hour or so, we'd park and be handed matching orange hi-visibility safety jackets before heading out and hoping for the best. It did not always work out. But eventually, I found myself standing on a frozen beach, watching a massive green eye rise from the sky above me and then fade away. It was as hazy as the previous night's encounter, but it was alive and crackling on the edge of my hearing. You lost it in the blink of an eye. It got shy again when you pointed an iPhone camera at it. The guides, on the other hand, had single-lens reflex cameras and tripods, and we all came home with photos of ourselves glowing in bright green light that we could never have seen with our own eyes. We emerged from the woods around two a.m. that night, and our guide joked, "There are bears in these woods, but don't worry, they've never eaten anyone yet!" He then focused his attention on me briefly. "I wonder if pregnant women send out different pheromones, though." At the time, I realised I was trembling so badly from the cold that my arms were twitching beside me, and I was about to puke all over the lovely snow. If my pheromones didn't entice the bears, this may. I returned to the bus and slept off the rest of the night's excursion, fantasising about those lovely emerald swirls of light. I was practically addicted by that stage, feeling compelled to collect my lifetime supply of ionising plasma while I still had the chance. We took a bus north and then boarded a scarlet ship heading south through the fjords. I stood on its terrace, watching a pinkish sliver of light ripple above my head, as if the wind had caught the curtain of an open window. There appeared to be so many magnificent aurora permutations, yet they were all fleeting, as if the line between your dreams and reality was blurred. It was a feeling similar to pregnancy: the notion that something very real is present one minute, followed by the realisation that all you know about it is a daydream the next. At the end of my vacation, while looking for my forgotten mittens in a hotel lobby, I observed a small glimmer of the aurora above the harbour and imagined it had always been there. It is just waiting for me to figure out how to view it.

We did not just roam around at night. We took a minibus to Whale Island one morning to witness a Sámi family with their reindeer. The road led us across the snowy Lyngen Alps, behind which the sun rose, turning the mountains pink. We travelled through fjords where people were swimming despite the extreme weather, and I began to understand the link between beauty and hardiness that existed in this freezing environment, as well as how these people worked hard to maintain their relationship with the sublime.

When we arrived, we were handed snowsuits and massive Davy Crockett caps, which we were told to wear over whatever we were wearing. Then we were escorted inside a lavvu, a traditional temporary Sámi dwelling shaped like a tepee, where we sat around a fire and regretted the cold. Because I couldn't find a snowsuit baggy enough to fit, everyone in the group figured I was pregnant, and I gained an uncomfortable degree of celebrity. The women in our company grumbled and tutted around me, asking aloud why I'd travelled all the way out here in this state. I made a poor joke about how sitting is the same everywhere. I was cautioned at least sixteen times that week to avoid huskies, and I was definitely asked a hundred times whether I was watching One Born Every Minute. I was, but I feigned not to be in order to escape the traditional childbirth group therapy session. I did nothing of the sort and was relieved to be let out at some point to meet the reindeer.

The Sámi are a people whose homeland spans the north of the peninsula where Norway, Sweden, Finland, and Russia now meet, despite the fact that they have resided there for approximately ten millennia. As nation-states emerged around them, the Sámi were persecuted by the many governments that came along the way. They must demonstrate ownership of the land on which they have resided since time immemorial. Despite the fact that Sweden, Norway, and Finland officially acknowledge them as an indigenous people with their own devolved legislatures, significant injustices continue. There are no such safeguards in Russia, and the Sámi remain vulnerable to forcible expulsion and incursions into their territory, as they have for a long time. Theirs will always be a perilous position: a civilization made up of distinct cultures, living in a land within a territory, seeking to preserve a way of life that most modern Europeans would find repulsive. The Sámi have traditionally survived through hunting, fishing, fur trapping, and, most significantly, reindeer herding. Reindeer are so closely associated with Sámi culture that Norwegian law grants them sole ownership of the animals. They are used for food, transportation, and clothing, and were once accepted as cash as an alternative to monetary taxation. Earmarks are tiny cuts done in the ears of reindeer by Sámi herders, and each family has its own distinct design. They are well-known for their in-depth understanding of their herds and life cycles. Their faith is animistic, with the notion that souls can be discovered in a wide range of animals, plants, and landscape features. Sámi sieidis include bears, ravens, seals, water, winds, and seidis, which are unusual rock formations that stand out in the surrounding environment. A number of gods and spirits are honoured, ancestors are present in daily life, and specific locations are designated as significant to individual families. Reindeer, understandably, play a big role in the Sámi imagination. Beivve, their sun goddess, travels across the sky in a ring of reindeer antlers every day, giving fertility to the ground. During the winter solstice, she would be sacrificed along with a white female reindeer. As the sun rose, she was showered with butter gifts, which were placed on doors and melted in her presence. Meanwhile, mythology describes the Meandash, or reindeer people, as being formed by a shaman lady with the ability to shift into either a human or a reindeer. She is so intelligent and ancient that, like the reindeer, it is thought she lived before time. My expectations of the reindeer were significantly more simplistic, based only on what I'd learned from a lifetime of Santa Claus. They were wilder than I had expected up close, with erratic head motions and eyes that roved in their sockets as we approached, displaying their whites. Some had mossy fur dangling from their horns. "That's because they're supposed to fall off soon, before spring," said Trine, our host. She added that reindeer bulls compete for females by shedding their antlers at the end of the mating season, when winter arrives. They soon grow another pair, but these are frail and fragile for a few months, with blood vessels near the surface, and do not fully harden until the autumn, when the animals resume fighting. Females, sometimes known as cows, shed their antlers in a distinct cycle. They have their young when the male antlers are softest, so they keep their own antlers for a longer period of time to protect their calves from predators. That implies that the ragged-antlered deer were all females who flaunted their toughness like a crown.

Later, we each rode in a sleigh towed by one of them—my reindeer had been carefully chosen for its kind nature, but it was nevertheless a bumpy voyage over the snow and around a frozen lake, all while sitting on reindeer skins. After that, we headed to the lavvu for some reindeer soup to help us get over the cold. As I finished my meal, Trine rushed over to refill it. "You do not have your antlers, Mama Reindeer," she added. "You don't have any antlers," "so we must fill you up with soup instead." I fell into tears because she had articulated something I couldn't till now: pregnancy made me feel as if I lacked a kind of defence and couldn't fight for myself. The reindeer realised what was necessary to survive the winter. No, I didn't.

In Troms, I discovered that magnificent things can survive in the dark, cold polar night, but I also realised that, no matter how hard I tried, I just had no defence against the changes in my life. My antlers were missing. I had skittered over to a distant country to persuade myself that everything would be alright, but all I saw was my own desperation mirrored in the ice.

But it was also there that I confronted my own limitations and the future that lay ahead of me. I realised that I was not invincible at this time in my life, and that it would not last forever. I learnt how to submit and rest. I learned how to daydream. I created photographs that I imagined showing to an unknown future person, saying, "Look, here you are under the northern lights."

Few of us inherit the Sámi's vast and intricate mythologies—the sensation that the world is alive around us and that ancestors are keeping a benign watch over us, existing in the very rocks we stand on and the wind that blows. Most of us must create our own, if we even contemplate it. During my time under the aurorae, I considered the first mythological gift I could bestow upon my son: the seed of his own distinct lore. You, who were so powerful that I expected you to absolutely overpower me, reached the Arctic Circle before you were even born...

We chose the first gift we'd ventured to buy for him before leaving: a small plush polar bear, soft and white, standing on all fours. Troms is still his name.

CHAPTER 10
IT'S SNOWING

I've often heard of snow nostalgia, or how we imagine our childhoods to be snowier than they were. I've had a yardstick to measure this since my child was born, and I can confidently say that we didn't have much more than a scattering over his first six years of life. We waited with the impatience of the children. Every year, at the start of the winter season, we would buy him a pair of warm padded trousers and a matching jacket, which he would hang on the coat rack alone. Bert describes snow as a mythological beast, similar to the dragons he would make if he could. He aspires to meet it someday, but realises that this is an unachievable goal. I'm sure I've never witnessed a snowy Christmas, but I do recall winters—probably more than one—when our town was cut off by snow, with the power out and supplies in the small shop running low. My mother told me about an elderly woman clutching the bread as if we were about to starve. When the milk cart finally made it through, folks gathered on their front steps to watch. We had so much snow in 1987 that the drifts on the side of my school's lane towered above the car. Those of us who made it were given soup at breaktime to keep us warm—oxtail or tomato soup served in an orange plastic beaker. I was permitted to wear a white roll-neck sweater beneath my shirt and tie, and my mother agreed to let me wear my moon boots if the instructors objected. Our house developed so many long and thick icicles that we started documenting them, measuring them with sewing tape (one was four feet long, I believe) and snapping them off to shoot in the bath. Because we didn't have central heating, I had to dry my snow-soaked clothes in front of the gas fire in the back room, and we were worried that the Calor Gas heater would sputter out before the thaw. I cannot say I was bothered. I was amazed by the harshness of our winter and its incredible ability to alter. I did not want it to end. I still have some of that attitude towards snow. I can't muster the mature harshness toward a snowfall, full of resentment for the inconvenience. I like the inconvenience in the same way that I enjoy a bad cold: a compelling disruption to daily life that compels you to pause for a while and move outside of your usual routine. I enjoy the visual transformation it produces, the recoloring of the environment in brilliant white, and the way the rules shift so that everyone meets one another as they pass. I enjoy how it alters the light, the purplish clouds that appear before it arrives, and how it emerges from behind your curtains in the morning, emitting a diffuse whiteness that can only be snow. When I step outside during a snowfall to catch the flakes on my gloves, I love the feel of fresh snow underfoot. Except in the snow, I am rarely youthful and playful. It sends me into reverse.

Snow inspires awe in the face of a power greater than ours. It illustrates the aesthetic concept of the sublime, in which greatness and beauty merge to completely overwhelm you—a small, sensitive person. I had no experience with snow before having a child. I encountered it one year when driving a chest of drawers to the municipal landfill, which was fine until I tried to brake at the main road intersection and veered right over two lanes, slow and stately as a cruise ship. Fortunately, no other vehicles were on the way. I encountered it on the Eurostar to Paris, where it stalled the lines and detained us for a week, forcing us to shrug and spend additional time sitting in luxurious cafés. I first saw it when I moved to Whitstable and found myself racing onto an empty beach to see what the waves looked like crashing over snow. Bert, on the other hand, has acted as a snow mascot. I have a photo of him as a newborn, strapped to my front and wearing an earflap cap as I cross a two-centimetre gap, but he can't recall it. I bought him a sledge as soon as he learned to walk, knowing that if I waited till the snow fell, the entire town would have sold out and we'd be left with tea trays. It lay unused and ruined in the back of the shed after we stacked other items on top of it. A sledge is a white elephant in Whitstable, which enjoys a mild microclimate. I've considered driving him to watch a snowfall in a nearby town or even a neighbouring county, but I'm quite sure blizzard tourism qualifies as parental carelessness.

He finally got his snow last winter. One Sunday morning, at seven a.m., the flakes began to fall across the garden, and I dashed upstairs to wake him up to observe. We put a coat and cap over his pyjamas, thick socks, and wellies on him and sent him out into the garden to play in the pathetically thin layer that had gathered across the lawn. By the time we completed breakfast and were ready to go outside for a second dose, the pavements were already slushy and the gutters were overflowing with ice melt. I wondered if that was the last snowfall we'd get until the following year.

But then it happened: it was predicted overnight in the weather forecast (which we didn't believe), but it was clearly there when we got up the next morning. This time, it was thick in the garden, hiding all the weeds and bald grass and making the entire area pleasant. We put on our winter clothes and went to the beach, where the snow formed enormous marshmallows on top of the sea wall and the grey sea had turned to slush. We rolled snowballs on the seashore and created a snow seagull with a twig beak and cockleshell bow tie. Later, we bought a new sledge (there were plenty on hand) and went to Tankerton Slopes, which was packed with laughing kids with red cheeks pelting down the slope and staggering back up. We observed four young lads sharing a kayak that had sailed off the seawall and crashed onto the beach below.

A snow day is a hectic day, an unexpected holiday in which everything is turned upside down. This one contains hints of both Halloween and Christmas. It was simultaneously crazy and cosy, irreverent and lovable. Another liminal zone, another place of intersection between the ordinary and the supernatural. Winter looks to be full of them: fleeting moments to deviate from the norm. Snow is beautiful, but it is also an expert con artist. It opens up a whole new world for us, but the moment we accept it, it disappears. When I see snow, I think of Narnia. C. S. Lewis captured the Platonic ideal of snow in a variety of ways, including a gorgeous thick white coating over pine forests and pleasant villages. After creeping into a wardrobe with the heavy fur coats they require to endure it, the children witness a quick transformation. Snow is a welcome surprise in The Lion, the Witch, and the Wardrobe, at least for a brief while. The narrative reverberates with the joys of snow: the lamppost's yellow light reveals the purity of its whiteness, and we are confronted with a world in which every ugliness has been banished, or at least concealed. Snow allows the children to really appreciate Mr. Tumnus and the Beavers' kind hospitality, as they are shielded by the glow of the fireplace and given nursery food. The inhabitants of Narnia give warmth, which is enhanced by the cold outside. There's little doubt that we should recognize the White Witch's malice right immediately, but we also can't overlook her glamour.

Hers is an icy beauty, piercing and crystalline, a testament to the fortitude required to bear the cold's toll. Edmund is tempted by her Turkish delight, which offers him superhuman abilities. I've always thought she carries a Christmas message: the sweets and food, the promise of gifts, but also the way it forces children to dance with their own hunger for a season, encouraging them to seek worldly goods while also chastising them for wanting them too much and too quickly. She is the adult half of Christmas seen through the eyes of a child, with a little bitter tinge that children can't help but notice as adults lecture them on the need to change their demands, on the sacrifices adults must make to carry out their midwinter visions. She is the mother who dresses up for a party where children are not permitted, leaving the house decked out in exotic makeup and perfume; the grownups who loiter at the card table with drinks on Christmas Eve, their comfy chores accomplished. She represents the grown-up pleasures that children have yet to experience.

However, The Lion, the Witch, and the Wardrobe is not the only book that associates snow with the beginning of adulthood. The Dark Is Rising by Susan Cooper begins with a heavy snowfall enveloping Will Stanton's family cottage on his eleventh birthday. Soon, he has time-travelled to a realm of magic and prophecy, as well as the rising threat of evil, and he is the only one capable of saving the world. Will matures in the snow. The same icy segue takes us to John Masefield's The Box of Delights, where the young hero Kay Harker witnesses a similar seepage in time during a Christmas holiday. The snow not only creates a fantastic cage in which the person can move rapidly or slowly, but it also combines the ancient pagan world with the blinding certainty of Christianity. Time has lost its linearity in the snow, and a rich past is evident. Most crucially, a young child is compelled to take the role of an adult when his parents and guardian are absent unexpectedly. Snowfall is the spark that causes tables to turn in children's literature. It creates a setting in which typical adult defenders are quickly made ineffectual and introduces a cosmos in which youngsters are agile and wild enough to thrive. The mighty are brought down in the huge struggles young children face, while the weak ascend to prominence. This can only happen in the dead of midwinter, when the world's typical features have vanished. Snow defeats the usual. It brings the everyday grind to a halt and limits our ability to meet our basic obligations. Snow gives the children unexpected freedom, transforming them into daredevils who can withstand the cold.

They sense the blossoming of their own might in this sparkling white space. Bert did not want to go outside to play on the second day of the snowstorm. He couldn't bear the layers of clothing anymore. He refused to put on his hat. He loathed the way the wind burned his face. We watched The Lego Movie, and it wasn't until sunset that I got him to take advantage of the opportunity and go outside again. We strolled down to the shore, which was now illuminated by ethereal pink light. Dog paw prints littered the snow, and the birds appeared to cling to the bare shingle strip beneath the tideline. They're used to picking up abandoned leftovers from adjacent chip shops and seafood cafes, so this must have been a difficult week for them.

The shallows were thick and shifted strangely along the water's edge. The salt water was nearly frozen, like slush. Bert splashed through it in his wellies, but his feet quickly turned chilly, so we had to come home. Whitstable's water has fully frozen over three times in recent memory: 1929, 1940, and 1963. Even more frequently, the calm waters of the harbour sparkle. Photographs from 1963 depict the seafloor as a wasteland of fractured ice, reminiscent of a particularly brave northern expedition. The sea froze in waves near Minster on the Isle of Sheppey, as if an unseen hand had stopped them in mid-undulation. Locals drew sledges across them, as if reenacting an ancient frost fair. I keep hoping that the same event would happen again one year just so I can see it, but I'm afraid it won't. Our frigid spells pass quickly. When we awoke the next morning, there had been a freeze, but not the one I had anticipated. We must have slept overnight, which was not warm enough to melt the snow but wet and cold enough to leave a thin layer of ice on everything. We broke through the thin layer of snow on top. The bare sections of the pavement appeared to have been coated with glass. Every fence post, streetlight, and automobile was sparkling. Eden Phillpotts referred to the weather as "ammil," which is a corruption of "enamel." In "A Shadow Passes," published in 1918, he described it as "a very rare winter phenomenon produced by the sudden freezing of heavy rain or fog." It differs significantly from frost in that it presents the world of trees, stones, and heather as if it were thinly coated in translucent glass. If the sun shines on such a view in the morning, the earth appears to be an unusual and beautiful dream. The piling of ice on top of snow feels less like a dream and more like a return of conflict. We were tired by the time we arrived at the beach. The weather was no longer a friendly and generous provider of a winter haven. It had become sour. The sky above us was a furious grey, and the sea was an ugly khaki, buffeted by a harsh wind. Everything around us appeared harsh, unwelcoming, vicious, and dangerous. The snow was now only complicating our lives.

"I want the snow to stop," Bert responded.

"Yes," I answered. "A couple of days was plenty."

"I don't miss it," my friend Päivi Seppälä says. "It's a nuisance."

We're drinking coffee in the kitchen of her baby, the LV21, a brilliant red floating lightship converted into an arts centre by her husband, Gary Weston. It is anchored in Gravesend on the Thames, where a beluga whale, a migratory species from the Arctic, has recently made its home. It's tempting to believe that the whale has moved there to join Päivi, who has also relocated south of her native area.

Päivi is from Hamina, a small town in Finland on the Baltic Sea between Helsinki and St. Petersburg. Hers is a land nestled between the sea and the lakes, where winter reigns for six months of the year.

"When the snow comes, it's actually a bit of a relief at first," she told me. "The short days make everything seem so dark. It suddenly snows, like if someone turned on the lights."

Her family opens separate winter draperies, not to remain warm, but to let in the light reflected from the snow cover. Everything becomes focused on letting the outside world in rather than keeping it out.

Päivi perceives living in the heavy cold as full of problems and frustrations rather than winter romance. With snow on the ground for three months of the year, schools never close for cold weather (though children are allowed to play indoors if the temperature falls below -25°C), and taking time off work is not an option. Everything must keep running. This requires spending hours each morning digging out and warming up the automobile, as well as bundling up in winter clothing for even the shortest trips. Simple activities are time-consuming and harmful. Roads are made across the frozen lakes, but these are not always safe, and individuals, including Päivi's father and sister, have fallen through the ice at various times. Everyone has warm coats and boots in their cars just in case. The possibility of becoming stranded exists. Mobile phones use all of their energy to stay warm, and their batteries run out so quickly that they are nearly useless.

You take vitamin D and attempt to spend as much time outside as possible. Some people cycle with snow tires, while others ski. In the winter, keeping the house warm might cause your electricity bill to skyrocket to the equivalent of £2,000 per month. It's a necessary evil, yet it causes indoor air to become so dry that your skin turns to scales. You drink lots of coffee to remain awake and avoid succumbing to the drinking culture that harms the health of so many Finns. When you go out for the night, you must pledge to abide by the policy of "no man left behind." It is not an option to pass out in the snow. You grow up hearing stories about people who perished as a result of one bad decision made after a night out in the cold.

It's a joy for me to think of snow as a little bit of light relaxation. Snow is simply exhausting for those who have to deal with it. British stupidity in the face of a brief cold spell is a national joke, but it's also a result of not having to make the effort to deal. We handle snow as if it were a dirty weekend and then return to work, moaning about the slush.

"So is there nothing you like about snow?" I'm slightly deflated, I say.

"Oh yes," Päivi says. "When it's really cold, the snow makes a lovely noise underfoot, and the air seems to be full of stars." I miss being able to hang my laundry to dry."

"Does it actually dry?" I inquire.

"Not really," she admits, "but it smells amazing afterwards." Rather than washing your woollens, hang them out to destroy the bacteria. It's beneficial to them."

"And you sauna?"

"We do, indeed. And then we tumble around naked in the snow. You get a garden full of obnoxious snow angels. We occasionally made a hole in the ice to dip our feet into the water. You put down rag rugs to keep your feet warm. I have to yell in order to get in, but it's... invigorating. We've got candles, ice cream, and coffee. We all have coping strategies."

I recall Hanne telling me about how snow draws you closer to your family, forcing you to find moments of collective leisure in tight quarters. Summer only scatters us. In the winter, we speak a common language of comfort: candles, ice cream, and coffee. Sauna. Clean laundry.

"But you wouldn't go back?" I ask.

"No. This"—she gestures to her boat, which has taken years of hard work to restore, involving huge social and financial sacrifices—"is much easier."

Her adolescent niece, who is visiting from Hamina, walks in at that very moment. "Tell Katherine what you think about the winter," Päivi says to her.

"I hate it," Luna says. "I hate the cold."

"How many times has your car gotten stuck now?" Päivi asos.

"Twice," Luna says. "Once upon a time, I had to be dragged off the ice by a tractor." I once spent an hour pulling my automobile out of the snow."

"And she's only just passed her test," Päivi adds, her eyes rolling slightly.

CHAPTER 11
COLD WATER

For the past three years, I've taken part in Whitstable's annual New Year's Sea Swim. It goes like this: a swarm of us linger around the beach for as long as we can get away with it before going in, screaming, and running back out. It's over in a flash. I merely participate so I can say I did it. First, there's a sophisticated maze of planning: the first year, I arrived with both a rash guard and a wetsuit, with a swimming costume underneath, sea shoes, and a woollen cap. I eventually got rid of the rash vest. I bring three large towels, a dressing robe, a tracksuit, a flask of hot tea, and a premixed Bloody Mary for the aftermath. I'm only in the water for around 15 seconds. The best part is getting back into my clothing and appreciating my own bravery. My dream of living on the coast included swimming all year. In my early twenties, I read Iris Murdoch's The Sea, the Sea and imagined myself as the kind of hardy spirit who got into the water every day and blazed a few determined strokes through the waves. What was the point of being there? For the first year, I excused myself because we had arrived in town in November, and it seemed like a bad idea to start when the water was already so cold. I reasoned that it was best to begin in the summer and gradually acclimatise. Then I will not notice. I swam a little this summer, but nowhere near enough. I couldn't get a handle on the tides. After a few months, we moved from our leased beach property to a more affordable five-minute walk away. It meant that on several occasions, I put on my swimsuit and headed to the beach, only to find that the sea was so far away that I'd have to wade through acres of muck to get there. Once or twice, I attempted this feat only to find myself ankle-deep in water. I realised I needed a tide table, but instead of buying the basic ones sold in practically every local pub and café, I was able to get a more complex one from an art museum. If I aligned a wheel and checked it against a complex table, it revealed the tides over the entire south-east coast. It was the most frustrating inconvenience. I ultimately gave up. My friend Emma asked if I would accompany her on her own New Year's swim this year, as part of a bucket list of goals she hopes to complete around her fortieth birthday. I was supposed to be able to provide the advantage of my cold-water expertise, and I didn't want to say it was ineffective. The fact that it was only the two of us made the entire experience feel quite different. I handed her my spare wetsuit and assured her she'd be OK. At the same time, I had a bodily aversion to joining the sea. I got the idea that swimming (if you can call it that) in close proximity to the other thrashing bodies over the previous few New Years had a warming effect that we wouldn't have experienced on our own. And jumping into this pool would need all of my willpower. Last year, I had no option but to follow the crowd.

We ended up driving the short distance to the beach, thinking we could easily get back in the car and turn the heat up to full blast when we were finished. I'm not going to lie: I had memorised hypothermia signals just in case. We crashed onto the beach, facing the water. It was 6 degrees Celsius outdoors and pouring. The water's temperature was closer to 3 degrees Celsius. The sky was a uniform white, and the sea was a turbulent grey. "Right," I replied, "come on." The sooner we do this, the sooner we can get home."

We sprinted, tripping over the shingle and into the waves, emitting a battle cry that turned into a squeal as we approached the sea, Emma counting down three, two, one. I got up to my thighs in the water before deciding to swim a few strokes. That's when the cold struck: a big harsh wall that drew air from my lungs. It was so plain. So vicious. I made a terrible attempt at a breast stroke, which was impossible. The frigid water drew me in like a brittle rubber band. It reminded me of fear. I had no room to move or draw in the air. It seemed as if the sea had grabbed my hand in an icy fist. I regained my footing and dashed back out of the water, Emma hot on my heels. Something strange happened after that, as we stood on the beach, towels piled around us and a cup of hot tea in hand. Looking back at the water, I felt tempted to do it all over again, to relive those crystalline seconds of intense cold. My veins shone with blood. I was convinced that I could defeat it the second time and stay in that cold claw for a little longer.

"That was brilliant," I said.

"The effect begins as soon as I reach the shore. My body anticipates what's coming and starts to warm up. Just thinking about going into the sea boosts my body temperature from 37 to 38 degrees.

Dorte Lyager is seated in her car, her face glowing after what I suppose is the result of a swim, as I talk to her on Skype. She is an experienced cold-water swimmer who swims in the sea all year in her hometown of Jutland, Denmark's northernmost point. And she does it to survive.

"Seven to eight degrees is the ideal temperature," she adds. "I can put my head under and feel completely immersed in cold water." "Everything is swept away as I rise again."

Dorte is a member of the Polar Bear Club, a group of year-round swimmers. Every morning at seven o'clock, roughly twenty of them meet to swim. These clubs can be found all along Denmark's coast, and many of them have changing rooms as well as saunas to warm up afterward. Dorte has been a member for three years, and despite the severe circumstances that brought her to the club, she has become a shining example of the benefits of spending time outside in the cold. I called Dorte after reading her blog, which is filled with breathless tales about briny highs, since I had the impression that life had taught us both the same thing. We've both found a way to persevere by enjoying winter rather than resisting it. "In October 2013, I was at the end of the road," she said. "I had been sick with recurring hypomania and depression for the previous ten years." I have tried every medication conceivable. My psychiatrist repeatedly told me that it was all about achieving the right balance; the goal was to become rask. It is a challenging word. It suggests both "healthy" and "fixed." I had been waiting for the medicine to work for a decade. The shift happened when I stopped believing it was feasible.

Dorte reached a tipping point when she received a fresh perspective on her situation, which changed the way she thought about it. Feeling that her drugs were failing her again, she scheduled an appointment with her GP and the opportunity to meet a doctor she had never met before. He stated they could keep adjusting her prescription, but it would never solve everything. "This isn't about you getting fixed," he explained. "This is about you living the best life you can with the parameters that you have."

He was the first to say it, and it had a significant impact. Perhaps a year or less ago, she would not have been prepared to hear it, but she was today. It should have been terrible to accept that she would always be bipolar; after all, it was already wrecking havoc with her health and happiness. But for Dorte, this was not the end of her hopes, but rather an invitation to eventually adapt to what she needed. "No one had ever told me, 'You need to live a life that you can handle, not one that other people want.'" Begin saying "no." Do only one item each day. "A maximum of two social gatherings per week. I owe him my life."

We'll soon be having the kind of frenetic talk reserved for old friend reunions rather than first-time internet contacts with complete strangers. But my reflection can be found thousands of kilometres over the North Sea. Our experience with winter pulls us in. I instantly interrupted to tell her my own tale of being diagnosed with Asperger syndrome and eventually realising that I couldn't fight my way out of it or find a therapy that would assist me. The label's permanence—having a brain that just happened to work in a certain way—was my rescue. I needed to change. I had no option but to give up. Only pretending to be like everyone else broke me. Dorte, like myself, had always been the type who fixed everything for others. She wasn't just scraping by. She was attempting superhuman acts of generosity by organising events and activities for all of the neighbourhood mothers, overburdening her family life with events and activities, and constantly filling her house with people. She was abruptly instructed to look after herself in order to survive. She initially discovered a public spa and began visiting twice a month to relax. It was expensive, but she understood she needed to learn how to look after herself. She'd sit in the sauna, then leap into the frigid plunge pool, repeating the process. However, after a few trips, she found she preferred the cold over the calming heat. Something was happening in her thoughts, making everything appear clear and peaceful for the first time in years.

"When I'm stressed, it's as if my brain has turned to porridge and is spewing out of my ears." My bipolar meds never completely eliminated it. "Cold water works." Dorte, a biologist by training, began researching modern studies on her condition and discovered the work of Edward Bullmore, a Cambridge neuroscientist who believes depression is caused by brain inflammation. From this perspective, the cold's effect made sense. "I'm treating my brain like an inflamed joint," she went on to say.

Porridge-brain is something I'm all too familiar with—the feeling that your head is so full that everything comes to a halt. I'm intrigued by the idea that it can be treated so quickly with ice, but I'm concerned about what she does in the heat. Dorte tells me she got an old agricultural tank and goes to the local harbour to fill her trailer with 200 kilograms of ice. She fills it with 400 litres of water to create an ice bath with a temperature of around 3° to 4°C. It sounds like a lot of work to go through for something that most of us would find really uncomfortable, but Dorte has learned to want it. "At first," she says to me, "I could only manage to stay in for three minutes, but I've gradually built up to half an hour."

I'm visibly shuddering. "I love the feeling it gives me," she says. "I feel quite peaceful and relaxed. My inner voice does not say, "Get out!" like everyone else's does. Finally, it says. "At long last."

"Is it a distraction?" I speculate. "I mean, do you feel so uncomfortable that you forget everything else?"

"No!" she says. "I'm laughing and laughing while I'm in the water." All of my automatic thoughts halt. I always lower my head to prevent the cold from reaching my brain. I can't remember what was bothering me. A switch was flipped. "It is a physical phenomenon."

Dorte does not simply mean that she has identified a treatment procedure that relieves her symptoms. "It feels like I've been cured," she says. "A bipolar episode is defined as a manic high that lasts at least seven days followed by a depressive phase that lasts at least two weeks." I may feel depressed for a day and then go to the beach, and then I'll be done with it.

She is careful to clarify that she does not intend to diminish or dismiss the dangers she faces, or the likelihood that her illness will damage her again. However, she finds this form of control so effective—and delightful in the meantime—that it makes everything seem easy for the first time in her life. "I now think of it as mental influenza," she went on to say. "I don't push through, I don't put up a front, and I don't hold it in." I take a few days off and care for myself till I feel better. I go to the beach, eat well, cancel all of my appointments, and rest till I feel better. "I know what I'm going to do."

With this curriculum, she has accomplished something she could not have imagined a decade ago. "I became depressed again last year." I sobbed on the way to the beach and felt better on the way home. I went to see my psychiatrist, who informed me I was overmedicated and needed to cut back on my prescriptions. This made me concerned because I had never been without my medications before.

But we chose to attend a supported retreat, and the lower my dose, the better I felt." She is no longer taking any medication.

"It won't be a quick fix," she explains. "I'm still not the same as someone who didn't have a diagnosis to begin with." Swimming is only one of the changes I've made during this lengthy journey. I've reduced my sugar intake, scheduled alone time, taken long walks, and quit saying yes to everyone. I have lowered my working hours. All of these elements combine to generate a buffer, which I strive to keep as broad as feasible. When situations emerge that deplete my buffer, I must replace it. Maintaining health is almost a full-time job. But I lead a beautiful life."

On a February day, I am copied into a Facebook group with names I don't recognize, with the message "I think this is one for Katherine."

As I scroll through the speech bubbles, I notice that someone is attempting to organise a group of people who are willing to swim all year, regardless of weather. The majority of invitees respond something along the lines of, "You're completely insane, and I might be willing to join you this summer."

"Oh, yes, please!" I exclaim.

On the day after the first snowfall, I met Margo Selby on the beach. A small snowfall had fallen the day before, and as I stand on the beach in my bathing suit, I can see tiny drifts forming around the margins of the wave breaks in the dismal areas where the winter sun rarely shines.

"I'm so glad you came," Margo says. "I've been trying to go in on my own, but it's so hard to work up the nerve each time."

To say that the water and the ice beach are beneath my feet is an understatement. The seaweed is ice-covered. Frost emphasises the woodgrain of the breakwater. My breath creates an unpleasant white fog in front of me. I would have gone to the nearby café and got a hot chocolate if no one had witnessed my shyness. But now I'm grasping my wetsuit and considering whether to swim with my bobble cap on.

"I won't stay in for long," I tell myself.

"Neither will I," Margo continues. "I'm trying to build up to three minutes." I remove my coat and clothing, feeling the air bite my naked skin. Not only is the swim irrational, but so is the compulsion I feel to do it, the belief that it will help me, that it is important, and prudent. As I put on my wetsuit and shoes, I notice Margo is wearing nothing but a swimming costume and black socks.

"They're made of neoprene," she explains. "Five millimetres thick." She also has gloves, the kind that divers wear. "I enquired of some female channel swimmers. They told you needed to protect your extremities from... frostbite."

It's best not to think about frostbite just now. I stress that I won't be in the water for long, and we both turn to face the sludge-green sea. Getting into the water seemed to be impossible. But then we're both marching towards it with purpose, and my shins and thighs are drenched. I slide forward to immerse my body and realise we're both screaming without even realising it—not shouting, precisely, but singing through the pain of the cold, our air knocked out of us. This is not the place to be inhibited or tough. We both summon the joy of our suffering.

"Breathe!" shouts Margo, and I pull air into my lungs and determine that I can perform three breast strokes before getting out, so I do: one, two... It's barely two and a half minutes before I'm up and dashing out to huddle beneath my towel. I was in for about 45 seconds, although it felt like time was warped by the experience, so it could easily have been shorter. Margo swims with her head up, a determined expression on her face, and her cheeks puffing with exertion. I feel safe now that I've been in and out. I made it through. In retrospect, it is clear that remaining a bit longer would have merely been a matter of nerves.

Margo soon follows, standing next to me, drying off. The memory of cold tingles my flesh. "I think I have the measure of it now," I replied. "I came out because I didn't think I could stay in." But as soon as I got out, I saw that everything was alright. "I'd like to go back in."

"Tomorrow?" inquires Margo.

"Tomorrow," I promise.

The next day, I set a timer on my phone and discovered that if I ignore my fear of dying of hypothermia, I can stay in for nearly five minutes. I've done my research and know it's a slower process, which is strangely reassuring. I know I should get out of the water immediately if I start shivering, but even if I start feeling warm again. I'm generally safe as long as I'm experiencing the chill. On the second day, I discover that my thumb joints will give me a clear signal when it's time to give up: my bones experience the cold as severe pain in this most fleshless region of my body, which quickly subsides once I'm out of the water.

In Whitstable, you can only swim within two hours of the high tide, and the high tides are twelve and a half hours apart, so your swimming window varies by an hour every day. Our eleven a.m. swim on the first Sunday turned into a midday swim on Monday, then one, two, and three o'clock in the afternoon, until the short February days had us swimming almost in the dark. I was determined to make it through the week by swimming every day to push myself to acclimate, so I returned to the beach repeatedly and fought my urge to be warm and dry.

During that week, the sea temperature ranged between 5° and 6° Celsius, and I became accustomed to the strange body changes that occur in cold water. As you exit, your skin shines brilliant red, not the colour of a blush or a hot flush, but the characteristic deep orange of Heinz tomato soup. I've come to love that colour as a remembrance of having gone through something unlike anything else in my life. Once I'm comfortable and dry, I invariably begin to shiver in an unpleasant way. My body is visibly warming up again, something I haven't asked it to do in years. It makes me feel alive, and I am not afraid of it because Margo feels the same way. I purposely induced a crisis in my body to force it to reestablish balance. It feels amazing to be pushing my physical limits in such an interesting way. My veins quiver for hours afterwards, as if I've been infused with a great serum.

On the fourth day, I remove the wetsuit and swim in just my swimwear, and I'm surprised to discover that I'm fine. I've learned to accept the cold and breathe during the first thirty seconds when my chest feels constricted. On the sixth day, I stayed in for ten minutes straight, surprised by how quickly I had adapted. We rob together in the murky water, slipping into our pre-established pattern of joyful, stream-of-consciousness conversation. To an outsider, we must appear as high as two kites, trilling in awe of the cold.

"This is wonderful!" we exclaim. "This is amazing!" We are completely intrigued by our own courage, by how we have stepped out of the conventional world and into this other cosmos. Our town, with all of its fears and responsibilities, is rising on the other side of the coast, but we've built a barrier to keep it from reaching us for the time being. Nobody was able to bring us here. Nobody would do that. Dog walkers pause on the beach to look at us, pointing and shaking their heads. We've crossed a breathtakingly daring unstated line. We believe that the best spot to swim is Seasalter, because there, on the barren beach, distant from buildings and protected by a high seawall, we may strip naked and dry off. I don't have the body type to wear a bikini in the summer, but in the winter, I can expose my flesh to the sea and feel a part of its elemental strength.

Immersion in cold water has been shown to increase dopamine levels by 250 percent, a neurotransmitter that stimulates the brain's reward and pleasure centres. A recent study found that regular winter swimming reduced tension and tiredness, as well as negative states associated with memory and mood, and improved swimmers' overall sense of well-being. It's no surprise that we felt great, but the effects seemed to be more than just physiological. Getting into the sea on days when the temperature was nearing zero was a show of defiance in the face of our own challenges. We felt more resilient after engaging in a resilient activity. That positive circle of resilience and feeling resilient kept us going.

I, who prefers to do things alone whenever possible, realised that this was only possible because of a contract between us. The anxiety of getting into the water—or even getting to the beach—never went away, but having a partner in crime made it harder to refuse. We challenged each other to find half an hour in our schedules to swim and reminded each other, as we stood in our swimming suits with goose pimples, that once we got in, we actually enjoyed ourselves. It was always tough to believe, but we took a leap of faith together.

Margo once said, "Of all the things I do in my day," "this is the only time that I don't think I ought to be anywhere else."

Extreme cold pulled us both into the most clichéd domain, the Moment, forcing our minds to shift away from dwelling on the past or future, or tiling over an unending to-do list. We had to take care of our bodies right away, while keeping an eye out for the cold. More than that, the sea presented us with a limitless number of opportunities to observe. Every day was unique—sometimes ridged with waves, sometimes millpond-level. It turned pewter under a clear sky, but rough grey under storm clouds. After a few calm days, the sea looked as clear and blue as the Mediterranean. Black-headed or herring gulls occasionally bobbed by us, a cormorant swooped by, and a swarm of sanderlings flitted low over the lake, tweeting. The odd dog swam out to greet us, and one day I watched helplessly as one stole my towel. There were days when the water seemed silky, and others when it was thick and mushy around the margins. We began to note how the sea would go slack at high tide, as if taking a breather before flooding again. The water was saltier before high tide and fresher thereafter. We assumed it was being diluted by the river.

Others were drawn in by our crazy excitement, and we became trainers, pushing people to tackle their fears, teaching them to breathe through the first few seconds and to leave when their thumbs ached. The sea acted as a shortcut to intimacy, and while we enjoyed our cold-water highs, we found ourselves spilling all of our current troubles. We swam alongside each other's financial, parental, and child-related issues. As soon as we entered the water, we dropped social etiquette and started talking. For a few moments, we let the cold ease the weight of our own personal winters, allowing us to openly express our darkest and most vulnerable thoughts. We spoke briefly, barely knowing one another's names, then wriggled back into our ordinary clothes and walked away, shivering slightly, feeling that sparkle in our veins. Our swims were brief, which provided an excellent opportunity to loosen and then tighten our tongues. We re-buttoned ourselves and returned home.

We made a bonfire on the beach as the sun went down at the end of the first month and dried off in its warmth while our children played. We sipped wine and toasted marshmallows, and we drew some new recruits: complete strangers who approached us and said, "Have you been in? Was it chilly? "How did you make it?""Can I join you someday?"

We greeted them with a smile.

CHAPTER 13
SURVIVAL

As a child, I had a glossy yellow hardback edition of Aesop's classic, The Ant and the Grasshopper. It featured the story of a laid-back grasshopper that spends the summer watching ants labour to save food for the winter. Meanwhile, he sunbathes and plays his guitar. In my opinion, he was a product of his time—the embodiment of the work-shy hippy, seemingly created in the decade before I was born to highlight the hazards of the desire to turn on, tune in, and drop out.

He has a little conversation with the ant in my recollection (which will remain a memory because I can no longer find the book) as he observes the hard work going on around him: Hey, dude, why so busy? Why not just enjoy the beautiful summer weather? The ant's remark becomes clear only when winter arrives and the grasshopper is starved and huddled against the oncoming winds: the wise have no time for frivolities. They are in the business of survival.

I now realise that this rendering was significantly larger than the Aesopian original, which is brutally compact. We don't get to watch the grasshopper's summer because we're placed immediately into his winter, where the ants are busy drying grain that they've been saving all summer. The grasshopper merely goes by, asking for food. The ants (who speak collectively) react frankly in George Fyler Townsend's translation, which was published in the mid-nineteenth century and is regarded as the canonical edition.

"Why did you not treasure food during the summer?" that's what they remarked.

"I didn't have enough leisure time," the grasshopper laments. "I passed the days of singing."

"If you were foolish enough to sing all the summer," you would be gnashing your teeth, "you must dance supperless to bed in the winter."

Even as a child, I was shocked by the ants' actions. The moral of the story seemed to be erroneous. I'm still in shock by the ants' aggression and the grasshopper's naive desire. This opposed all I had learned in school about Christian kindness. After all, he's merely done what a grasshopper should do: sing, and the ants have satisfied their own biological needs. At most, he made a tiny mistake that is unlikely to be repeated, but it always seemed to me that the ants had passed up a valuable trade—the entertainment of a singing grasshopper while they worked in exchange for a small amount of food in the winter.

When I consider the narrative as an adult, it takes on a darker tone. After all, the grasshopper does not overwinter; it survives entirely through genetics, in the form of eggs. As a result, the ants are not being asked to sustain an extra body during the winter; rather, they are denying the dying creature's final request. Did Aesop realise this? Is the tale an attempt to explain why grasshoppers disappear in the winter? Whatever viewpoint you pick, the ants are cruel, arrogant, and most likely genocidal.

But as I take my tongue out of my cheek, I can't help but feel the ants' attitude. It would have caught the Victorians' attention, and it undoubtedly resonated with many contemporary political views. The grasshopper is the universal vagrant—the layabout, the benefit scrounger, and the profligate who wastes his meagre wages on needless goods. People who believe the laws do not apply to them; fraudsters and crooks; mothers who, we are told, have infants solely to obtain public housing, or who sit at home on state maternity leave to avoid paying their fair contribution. The slackers and hangers-on, the adult children who refuse to leave their safe haven, and the millennials who are so consumed with purchasing avocado toast that they must rely on their parents' bank accounts. Economic migrants, refugees, and light travellers. This enormous, amorphous mass is beating on the door of honest people who work and always pay their expenses.

The grasshopper symbolism so many folk villains that it's hard to know where to start. His identity, I believe, varies with each age, social class, and town or city that faces new risks. Meanwhile, the ants are unmoving. They are typical, upright folks who conduct themselves appropriately. They save for rainy days rather than counting on the charity of others. They keep to themselves and take care of their own. They are a projection of how we frequently imagine we should live, but they are also a blueprint for a life that we have repeatedly failed to achieve throughout human history. The ants aren't real, at least not in big numbers; they're an if only. If only we could all become ants. If we were all this foresighted and responsible. If only the grasshoppers of the world could be dispatched in the same way.

If only I could provide you an alternative. If only life was so solid, joyous, and predictable that it produced ants instead of grasshoppers year after year. The truth is that we all have ant and grasshopper years—years when we can plan and save, and years when we require a little more help. Our underlying issue is not a failure to preserve enough resources to deal with grasshopper years, but rather a notion that each grasshopper year is an anomaly bestowed upon us solely because of our unique human shortcomings. I went on a walk behind the studio where I write in September. I essentially have a cabinet in an old farm building that is currently occupied by visual artists. I can't really justify taking up any additional space. All I need is a closet and a narrow shelf to store my laptop on. In any case, I spend more time walking than writing, exploring the farm and the fields beyond, where I can join the North Downs Way and walk to Canterbury in an hour. If I turn around, there's a line of small country pubs where I can sit for a while and pretend to collect my thoughts. But most of the time, I get a few moments of fresh air before returning to my screen. One path leads to a walnut orchard, while the other leads to a field of blackcurrant shrubs. And there are rows upon rows of apple trees: I went there that day, past the stacked wooden crates waiting to bring the fruit to market, through an area of green grass studded with the skeletons of innumerable umbellifers that had withered into brittle starbursts. The sun does not reach this spot until late in the afternoon, and a thick dew coats the ground, lighting up the spider webs and glossing the apples. I was on my way to a row of beehives, which was a frequent destination for my outings. I'd spent the summer listening to their conversation and seeing the bustling activity around them. But on that particular day, I noticed something peculiar. A sheet of newspaper was used to divide the hive in two, separating the top half from the bottom. The bees buzzed around it as if they were on invisible wires, pinging in their stiff flying patterns. Others clustered on the surface, crawling over the paper and investigating the seam created by their swarm. They were definitely curious. I, too, was interested. What good could a piece of newsprint do for a bee colony?

When I asked on Twitter, it appeared like everyone except me had the answer. The keeper was combining two hives to save the stronger bees from a weak colony whose queen was dying and would not survive the winter otherwise. The paper barrier allows these bees to join another queen without causing conflict, which could kill both colonies. The procedure is as follows: the beekeeper stacks a weak colony on top of a strong colony, with paper between. The bees sniff each other and start chewing on the paper, but by the end, the weaker bees have picked up the scent of their new queen and are less interested in fighting. When the beekeeper reopens the hive, nothing of the newspaper remains save a ring connecting the two hive boxes, and the two groups of bees will coexist peacefully. What sparked my interest, however, was a comment from Al Warren, a man who is so enthusiastic about beekeeping that he has persuaded his local primary school to house three of his hives. "I don't usually bother with the newspaper method," he told me. "Honeybees have quite surefire techniques of surviving the winter on their own." They are snow machines."

"When you think about bees," he subsequently says, "don't think of them as individuals." A bee colony is one superorganism. They behave as if they are one. And, while it's easy to image bees as summer creatures who buzz around flowers on hot days, their entire year is oriented in the opposite direction. The majority of a bee's activities is around ensuring that its colony survives the winter. They spend half the year preparing for it and the other half experiencing it. Every April, they emerge from their hive to start the process over again.

A honeybee colony has 30,000 to 40,000 bees, including one queen, a few hundred male drones, tens of thousands of female worker bees, and numerous eggs and larvae. The drones' primary function is to mate with the queen early in her life, after which she stores millions of sperm in her body and uses it to lay roughly two thousand fertilised eggs per day. All other tasks are carried out by the workers, who rotate through a series of responsibilities at various stages of their lives. When they are young, they keep the hive clean before moving on to a range of other activities based on their experience and expendability. They care for the queen, the larvae, and the young bees; they place nectar in the cells, manufacture wax to make new honeycomb, produce honey, and serve as guard bees. Because foraging is the most dangerous function of all, and older bees are disposable, it is their final role in life. We will most likely only ever see ancient bees sent out on risky missions to collect nectar for carbohydrates and pollen for protein. According to Al, the severity of a bee's sting is determined by its age, with older bees having substantially more lethal venom. Given the hazards they must face, it appears only fair.

Bees create this precisely balanced social order by functioning as cells inside a larger body. "You or I," Al adds, "have self-regulating bodies." Everything that keeps us alive happens without our conscious awareness. This is exactly what a hive does. It can sustain itself." Pheromones, vibration, and touch are employed to send colony requests to individual bees, allowing them to respond. Everything is automatic; the engine runs itself. It is also practically fail-safe.

Bees create honey to store carbs for winter. Because simply keeping the nectar would cause it to ferment, they develop an enzyme that turns nectar to honey by breaking its molecules and extracting the majority of the water. If a bee comes at the honeycomb and finds all of the cells filled, its expanding stomach produces wax, allowing it to immediately form a new cell. There is nothing left to chance in the hive. If a nurse bee dies, the larvae that remain emit a pheromone that induces each adult bee to retreat one stage, allowing the nurse role to be completed once more. Bees are sometimes seen as models of effective administration, despite being significantly more efficient. "If you cut your finger," Al goes on to say, "your body will deploy the appropriate cells to heal it." The same holds true for bees.

All of this immense effort—the combined efforts of an unimaginable number of bees—is geared firmly toward winter. They have discovered an ingenious way to remain warm. Honeybees may separate their wings from their flying muscles, shift into neutral, and then rev those muscles to become hot bees. In the winter, bees cluster together to conserve heat, and these cold-blooded insects take turns acting as miniature radiators, reaching 45°C, seven degrees warmer than the human body temperature. Even on the coldest days, a beehive's core temperature stays at 35°C. When one heating bee runs out of energy, the other takes over. The superorganism will persist till springtime. Honey fuels the entire process.

On this gloomy March day, I spot a few bees as I go around the orchards behind the artists' studios. The apple trees have yet to bloom, and the sunlight flows through the branches like water. Today is a challenging day. It's my final day in the small writing cupboard with yellow walls and a sense of purpose. I can't justify the rent since I'm too obsessed with my personal life to pretend I'm working. I'm wondering if this will be the winter that eventually takes me as I move, beating the bounds of a region I'm about to leave.

But then I go to the beehives and picture life stirring within. The wintering machine is softly and covertly going into motion.

I'm telling myself to be cautious even as I write about bees. It's all too easy to see them as miniature metaphors for humans, with the neat bustle of the bee colony serving as a model for all of us. I could easily fall for the tired old idea that bees are models of industry. Take after the bees.

Indeed, sociobiologist E. O. Wilson claims that we are more akin to bees than most people realise. He cites bees and ants as excellent instances of eusocial creatures—those who organise their labour jointly for the sake of their society—and says that humans exhibit similar behaviour, albeit in a different fashion. Humans may not have pheromone trails or anatomical specialisations like social insects, but Wilson contends that our willingness to cooperate is just as programmed.

Many philosophers on both the left and right have long been fascinated by the concept of the human machine—a natural order of things that could function as smoothly as a beehive if we could just break the awful habits we've established over the course of our existence on this planet. Whether you like military efficiency with no tolerance for individual complaints, or flat, egalitarian organisations in which everyone gets what they need rather than what they want, there's a beehive metaphor for you. Charlotte Perkins Gilman, for example, portrayed an idealised society developed by women in "Bee Wise," in which domestic labour was shared on a broad scale and women's devoted industry produced finer leather, cotton, and fruit. When it came to marriage, however, their men were required to "prove clean health—for a high grade of motherhood was the continuing ideal of the group." Benito Mussolini, on the other end of the political spectrum, frequently used the beehive to describe the ideal functioning of fascism. "It is usual to speak of the Fascist objective as the 'beehive state,' which does a grave injustice to bees," wrote George Orwell in The Road to Wigan Pier. "A world of rabbits ruled by stoats would be nearer the mark."

Before we get obsessed with the machinelike efficiency of the ideal human beehive, we must first understand bees' true lives. They are just fantastic. Their expertise, and, more importantly, their will to survive, is amazing. Their lives, however, are characterised by sharp efficiency. The area around my favourite beehive is littered with the remains of no longer useful bees—the most expendable, who were dispatched on the dangerous task of foraging; and male drones who were removed from the hive at the end of their useful lives—in the middle of winter.

We should not strive to be like ants and bees. We can derive enough awe from their sophisticated survival strategies without completely modelling ourselves after them. Humans are not eusocial—we are neither nameless units in a superorganism or simply cells that are expendable after our useful life is over. A social insect's life has nothing to do with us. Our lives take various forms. We do not progress in a straight line via defined roles like the honeybee. We are not constantly valuable to the rest of the world. We talk about the complexity of the hive, but human societies are incomparably more complicated, full of choices and mistakes, glory and sadness. Some of us offer highly obvious and elaborate contributions to the overall picture. Some of us are part of the world's ticking mechanics, the incremental wealth of modest actions. Everything is important. All of it contributes to the larger fabric that unites us. A single wintering in the eusocial hive would result in being driven out for the greater benefit. And it's possible that a bee can't recover. A human, on the other hand, can. We may drift through years feeling like a terrible presence in the world, but we are capable of returning. We can return to friends and family not only restored, but also capable of bringing more than we did before: greater insight, compassion, and an improved capacity to go deep into our roots and believe that water will be found. When it comes to humans, usefulness is a meaningless concept. I don't believe we were ever designed to consider people in terms of their utility to us. We maintain pets for the joy of caring for them; we willingly feed extra mouths and collect up waste in small plastic bags, proclaiming it pleasant. We direct our affection toward the most defenceless citizens of all—babies and children—for reasons unrelated to their future utility. We thrive on giving and receiving love. Our families and communities are held together by the most vulnerable people of our communities. It is how we survive. Our winters serve as a social glue.

The ants aren't entirely incorrect. Winter does bring its own labours, and plans might be made for future periods of famine that we cannot yet conceive. Of course, we've always been told to save, but many of us find it difficult to stretch our budgets that far these days. Even when we do save money, it is often of little use. My own savings were wiped out in one swift sweep when I was unable to work due to a miserable pregnancy, and then daycare cost more than I earned. It doesn't take much—just everyday items. The boundaries of adulthood are thin.

However, the winter operations are more complex than simply laying in supplies, which are then depleted until the summer refills them. We are called into the industry of the dark season, when there is nothing else to do but keep our hands going, while cooped up in our hives with chilly winds blasting at the ceiling. Winter is a season for quiet arts like knitting and sewing, baking and simmering, and mending and restoring our houses.

We want to be outside and active in the summer; in the winter, we are called inside, and here we respond to all the debris of the summer months, when we were too busy to take care of the necessary care. Winter is when I reorganise my bookshelves and read all the books I bought the previous year but never read. It's also the time when I reread old favourites for the joy of reconnecting with old friends. In the summer, I want big, splashy ideas and trashy page-turners, which

I can devour while relaxing in a garden chair or perching on one of the beach's breakwaters. In the winter, I want to chew on ideas in a pool of lamplight—slow, spiritual reading, soul nourishment. Winter is a season for libraries, with their muffled silence and the aroma of old pages and dust. In the winter, I can lose myself for hours in silent pursuit of a half-understood concept or historical detail. After all, there is nowhere else to be.

Winter allows for more time. "[T]here is nothing doing," writes Sylvia Plath in her poem "Wintering." "This is the time of hanging on for the bees," she explains after collecting their honey. It's currently in jars—six of them—on a shelf in the cellar, feeding on sugar syrup. Plath huddles in her basement during the winter emptiness, sifting out the remaining goods of prior occupants in her yellow torchlight and discovering only "Black asininity." Possession Decay." She is concerned about the hive's survival.

Plath did not make it through her winter, as every schoolgirl knows. She wrote "Wintering" near the end of her life, and it marked the end of her original draft of Ariel, her epic collection of love and agony, hope and loss, which was reedited for publication by her husband, Ted Hughes, following her suicide. "Wintering" takes us to the depths of the house, where "the black bunched in there like a bat." It has always been a tough poem for me to read. Its syntax is never excellent, in my opinion. Its sentences move between lines and stanzas, and the meanings get jumbled. I perceive a kind of disorder in it, as if we've been thrown into the middle of a mental process whose start and end we can't see.

Finally, in Hughes' interpretation of Ariel, we come to two poems that take on new weight after their author's death: "Edge," which at times appears to fetishize an already-occurring demise, and, as a coda, "Words," which finds a kind of stillness in death. However, this is a monument, set like a wreath after the author's death, presumably to make sense of such a tragedy; or, as feminist commentators have commonly asserted, to represent Hughes' ambition to dominate Plath's narrative even after death. Plath, in any case, never anticipated this outcome. As she put everything together, Ariel concluded on a much brighter note, the return of life: "The bees are flying." "They get a taste of spring." Plath sought a way to survive her winter through labour, namely women's jobs that required quiet hours at home. "Winter is for women," she says in the film "Wintering." It may be a period when feminine qualities shine, but I suppose she is also referring to the terrible times in which women can survive. It makes me wish she had more tasks to complete: more honey to spin, more bees to feed. Plath's advice to keep your hands moving in the winter was sound. According to a recent study, knitting can lower blood pressure as much as yoga and help chronic pain sufferers by creating serotonin. The nonprofit Knit for Peace conducted research into the health benefits of handicrafts and determined that they can help people maintain mental sharpness, quit smoking, and minimise loneliness and isolation in the elderly. They then contended that craft should only be available with a prescription. As I struggle through my own winter, I may not have time to complete the huge job that I desire, but I can keep my hands occupied. For the first time in years, I pick up my knitting needles and make a collection of deformed hats with proudly displayed dropped stitches. It feels good to contribute something, even if my contribution to the world is little. It allows me to see myself as a machine, fluid and efficient. And as I knit, I fantasise about one day owning my own beehive, spinning out jars of honey, and walking down the yard to my hive in the dead of winter to feel the hum of life inside.

CHAPTER 14

SONG

The robin starts to sing in the dead of winter.

In January, I observed one perched on the fence near to the bay tree, head inclined, with inquisitive small eyes on me. His breasts, which were a vivid orange rather than red, glowed like berries against the muted greens and browns of my dormant garden. He entered from next door to see what I was up to. I don't feed birds in my backyard since I have cats and wouldn't want to set a cruel trap. But my neighbour does, and I occasionally see blue tits and goldfinches wandering in from her hanging feeder, undoubtedly expecting me to be as kind as she is. Best of all, I receive the robin, who appears to have come solely to be kind. Robins are always the friendliest of birds, eager to hover around near gardeners in quest of worms. They appear to understand, more than any other bird, that we are less of a threat and more of a potential source of treasure. But they also seem captivated by us, with their heads cocked, as if asking, "What are you doing?" People throughout history have claimed to have had long-term friendships with robins. Some believe this is an illusion induced by all robins being friendly and looking the same, but some patient souls seem to have tamed their garden robin. Winter George is actor Mackenzie Crook's companion robin. "[H]e would think nothing of coming into the house," Crook wrote in The Telegraph in 2017, "perching on my shoulder and screaming at me while I was cooking for my family." He is educated and brave, and I am worried that one day he will not appear." Crook gradually attracted the robin while digging his garden, first by throwing worms and then coaxing him to remove a centipede from his fingers. Crook then went to the local pet store and purchased live mealworms to lure the bird to his back door. Winter George has become a permanent resident in his home, successfully producing clutches of chicks in his yard.

Unfortunately, I have yet to befriend a robin, but I always think of them as the bird family's cheerleaders. They have a knack of appearing when you are at your lowest point, as if to encourage you to keep going by reminding you that there is still magic in the world. I used to run (or try to run) along a long route between Whitstable and Canterbury, and there came a moment when I'd hobble to the top of a hill and feel like all I could do was pass out under the first tree. I'd slow down and wonder why I'd put myself through this, just to see a robin on the path ahead of me. I'd gasp, "Hello, old friend," and smile, and it was tough not to interpret him as a sign to keep going. He'd flit among the branches beside me until it was time to circle back and return home. Robins were first associated with winter in Victorian times, when they became the faces of a new Christmas card craze. The postmen who delivered them were dubbed "robins" due to their red uniforms, thus this could have been a joke. However, the cards most likely hint to an old connection between the robin and the birth of Christ. According to one common mythology, the robin got his red breast from viewing the infant Jesus in the manger. He saw that the fire had gotten dangerously near to the sleeping child and positioned himself between the flames and the youngster. His breast had been burned to a bright scarlet, which he passed on to his descendants.

However, the robin's link to Christmas may have more obvious origins as well. Simply put, robins seem to be present when other birds are not. They do not migrate, and their colourful plumage and friendly demeanour distinguish them from other birds. They sing even in the darkest months. Other birds call throughout the winter, but these are typically defensive notes intended to ward off predators. Robins, on the other hand, sing in full, sophisticated song during the coldest months, which is far too early to consider breeding. One ornithologist noticed that robins will sing as soon as the days lengthen, if they have enough energy. A well-fed robin— one that has grown enough fat to withstand the cold winter months and found a consistent source of nutrition to refill his reserves—will sing long before he expects females to respond to his display. In evolutionary biology, this is known as expensive signalling, a gesture that encourages remarkable power and vigour while also posing a risk to the creature. A robin sings in the winter because he can and wants the world to know about it—at least the female robins. However, he is also planning for happier days.

I lost my voice a year after having my baby. I'm not saying I absolutely lost it. Instead, it deteriorated and sagged around the edges. If I spoke for too long, it would crackle and then cut in and out, like a faulty microphone. My throat itches. I would cough ineffectively. My throat would finally whistle to silence as I swallowed and sipped water, desperately attempting to bring it back to life. I'd spent my entire life communicating, but now my voice was untrustworthy. My speech was being sliced up, and my words were being wiped out randomly. In daily conversation with people I knew, I would speak until my voice weakened and then wave my hand, hoping they would understand what I was saying. This was more difficult in the outside world. I found myself blaming colds and sore throats that I didn't have, without knowing why. I feel it is better to be viewed as temporarily useless than permanently useless. I would regularly avoid speaking in large groups with people I didn't know. It was pointless to begin. It is better to be silent than stammer and ramble till they lose interest. I felt like a living metaphor for the first eighteen months of fatherhood, with this lack of speech. Being a mother felt like becoming invisible, or at the very least semi-visible—noticeable enough to be admonished for forgetting to fold your pram on a bus (how, with a baby under your arm?) or taking up too much sidewalk space. But now you're a somewhat loathed species, caught in the middle and contributing to the world's overpopulation. Sitting around drinking coffee all day, or going to work while ignoring your mother's needs. Either/or. It makes no difference which option you choose. You've been wrecked. There were times when I felt no one would ever listen to me again, that everything important I had to say would be crushed under the weight of the bag on my shoulder, which was filled with diapers, food, wipes, and wardrobe changes. It seemed terrible that my voice would go away, but it also seemed entirely right.

One of the most terrible blows was that I couldn't sing anymore. It's easy to say, "Not that singing played a huge part in my life," but that's not true. Singing is not my profession or goal, but it has kept me going for as long as I can remember, from attempting harmonies with my mother in the car to warbling along to the radio as I cook. Throughout high school and university, I sang in choruses, and my low alto blended in with the other voices. Singing with others is a type of alchemy, an act of limitless magic in which you lose yourself and become a part of something greater. I've long relied on the stress-relieving effect of belting out half-remembered choir parts while driving alone in my car.

However, once Bert was born, my voice became too weak to sing. Even when I could play a few notes without crackling or croaking, there was no richness, no lovely volume to fill my lungs and relax my intercostal muscles. Singing was a gasping, breathless affair. Worst of all, my tune was gone. When I aimed for perfectly common notes, my voice simply faded away into murky timelessness. It felt like I'd lost a piece of my soul.

The conventional diagnostic criteria were not applicable. A camera was inserted into my nose and down my throat, but nothing was discovered: no polyps, no inflammation. There was no treatment or cure. That was all. I had lost my voice. It was just something that had happened, along with everything else that had ruined my sense of being a valuable presence in the world.

When a buddy suggested taking singing lessons, I laughed and said it was unnecessary. I had no intention of speaking in public again. However, she declined, claiming that it had nothing to do with singing. She believed that a good teacher may help me heal and maintain my voice in the future. This appears to be a common occurrence in the performing arts: voices become brittle and need to be restored or remapped. My voice was an asset, and I needed to handle it as other professionals would. Giving up was not an option. I was sceptical, but I was also drawn to the idea of spending an hour with a singing teacher, a piano, a quiet room, and a music stand. It sounded more pampering than a spa at the time. I sent a preliminary email to an instructor, explaining that I didn't want to learn to sing in particular, but rather to learn to talk again. I was surprised he reacted at all, but he seemed to think my request was entirely reasonable, though he did warn me that I would have to sing. I believed I could pull it off. We agreed on a time and date.

In the days running up to the session, I wondered if I could manage it. I was embarrassed to sing in public, especially in a room full of talented vocalists honing their craft, because I couldn't hold a single clean note. I thought I needed a barren, sterile clinic instead of the spotless living room in which I found myself standing, dry-mouthed, wishing for all the world that I could hide behind a curtain in shame while revealing the true horror of my voice. My tutor, Philip, struck me as a practical individual. I believe he knew straight away that I didn't want to sing: not in the middle of his living room floor, and not on stage. So we reviewed the fundamentals, including standing and breathing. I joked (as I'm sure he had heard a million times before) that I hoped I knew how to stand and breathe by now, but I wasn't sure. Standing and breathing felt far too much like the behaviours of a mature, capable adult with a place in the world.

So I learned to steady myself and breathe into my lungs. Then we tried to sing various scales. Philip played a middle C, and my voice rebounded off of it.

"See," I clarified. It was a hopeless case.

"Try B," Philip replied.

I could do B. The note was light and full of air, but I was able to hit both it and the A below it. I worked my way down the scale and back up again, discovering that I could nail that C after a flurry of other notes. It was there; all I had to do was slide on it sideways instead of facing it head on. My middle C had gone to hide. It's unusual to lose the note that everyone generally opens with, yet there it was. My scales began with an A and progressed to a few notes below that. We used to do run-ups on my C. If I envisioned it as a lengthy jump, I might be able to locate it. Sometimes you have to back up a few steps and restart.

In the weeks that followed, we worked on recovering the purity and loudness of my singing voice, which I had previously taken pride in. To keep my voice coming from my lower larynx, I learnt to stimulate the muscles at the base of my throat and imagine pulling an imaginary thread forward while singing. I learned to move from one note to the next in order to maintain my melody flowing like water. I didn't have the sore throat that I expected following my sessions. I felt a small section of my body relax and somewhat expand. I had sucked in the air around me and stopped being concave, crushed inward by existence. After a few classes, we had a talk about how I utilise my voice. I spoke all day, first to my family in the morning and then at work, using my voice to establish my place in the world. My voice was multitasking as the course leader of a creative writing program, attempting to inspire and thrill in the lecture hall, console in the privacy of my office, and assert solid, immovable authority in the face of an equally immovable university bureaucracy. In the meantime, I attempted to appear cheerful and pleasant in the corridors and canteens, but I was never permitted to nod and wave mutely as I desired. Even while I was silent, I was sifting through miles of email correspondence, usually with my teeth locked together in an attempt to appear clear, helpful, and kind. I was like an always-on lightbulb. I was brandishing my voice like a bludgeon, hoping to get everyone else to pay attention.

"Do you ever read your work aloud?" Phillip questioned.

"Sometimes," I confessed. "Not as much as I used to." The layers of reality underneath that: hardly one asked me anymore, and I no longer valued the attention or believed in my job. Nonetheless, I spent the entire day acting and dancing to other people's writing rather than my own, attempting (sometimes futilely) to invigorate classrooms already burdened by their own thoughts and worries. You cannot enter the classroom feeling unhappy or unwilling. You must sacrifice your own energy for the sake of your students', throwing your own reservations on the pyre of their lack of interest. You must reject the common pedagogical luxury of presuming your pupils are sluggish, disrespectful, or entitled. You do it instead, knowing that they are all suffering with their own pain, dread, work, and caregiving duties. You walk into your classroom and strive to keep the students entertained long enough to teach them anything useful for the future. I instantly saw my voice as a funnel into which I was putting all of my weight, hoping to produce a measured stream of words that would somehow solve everything.

"Do you know Under Milk Wood?" Philip inquired, and I said that, by chance, I had a brand-new copy on my desk at work, ready to support someone's dissertation. My copy of Richard Burton's 1954 recording of Dylan Thomas' drama is at home, tucked among my husband's towering piles of vinyl records. I find it unknown as a book, yet I'm always drawn to its undulating rhythms and dark comedy. Philip turned open his copy and set it on the music stand. "Read the first page," he added, and my voice faltered once more. Spring has arrived in the small village, with a moonless night, starless and bible-black skies, and silent cobblestone streets. I couldn't keep my breath long enough for those lengthy, meandering sentences. I could grasp them well enough in solitude, but when I spoke to them, I stumbled over them like a child trying to read. The first paragraph appeared to take a lifetime to disentangle. My speech was rough and percussive, dropping sentences at random and bouncing off others.

After I had made a mistake, Philip paused, and all of the people of the weary and perplexed town fell asleep. "Listen," he insisted, and he read it aloud, lightly bouncing on each emphasised syllable, letting the words flow over one another like waves on the water. "You have to approach it like a song," he advised me. Please take your time. Don't go after it; "just go with it."

I tried again, but this time more timidly, having recognized my own shortcomings so clearly. I believed I could read loudly and eloquently. But I hadn't so much read as crushed this lovely, flowing text. I approached it as if it were something to overcome, but it instead defeated me. I took a deep breath. It's Springtime...

I was slower now, and I was discovering more meaning, but I still felt like I was fighting three battles: my head, my breath, and this lethargic text. It exposed everything that was wrong in my life at the moment. I realised I was assaulting my immediate surroundings rather than fitting in with them. I couldn't keep up with the play's frenetic speed, whether inside or outside of a music class.

"Long Welsh vowels," Philip said, and things improved marginally. It took some practice to lengthen my own clipped Kentish phrasing without pastiching the accent, but the unhurried tone eventually settled in: hymning in bonnet, brooch, and bombazine black, that last k clicking like a wet log on a warm fire. It was surprising to read the line "trotting silently, with seaweed on its hooves, along the cockled cobbles" because the entire play is set on cobblestones that cannot be rushed. Listen. It's nighttime on the streets... Listen. It's late at night in the cold, small chapel. When you start utilising your voice as music, you have the right to expect attention. You have the right to respond, "Listen." My voice had faded along with my confidence, and regaining it felt like reclaiming my due place in the adult world. I was stuttering because I felt the urge to finish my sentences before being stopped.

My voice had already seen several alterations. As a child, I was applauded when I "spoke nicely" and punished when I dropped my t's in an effort to mimic the estuary English I heard all around me in my hometown of Gravesend. This precise method of talking was well appreciated at my primary school, though I was frequently chastised when, in reception class, I tried to imitate my teacher's Yorkshire accent. When I was eight years old, my family moved to a council estate, and the other kids mocked my poshness, so I tried to sound more like them, only to be chastised when I came home. At home and at school, I changed my voice multiple times. It was like being a tennis ball: at one end of the court, my voice was one thing, but it quickly switched to the opposite.

My voice altered again in my Rochester grammar school, which was full of girls who had studied for the eleven-plus exam and whose fathers were doctors and solicitors. For the first time in my life, I realised how poor we were and felt humiliated that we couldn't meet the financial needs of this public institution. When new blazers, sweaters with stripes around the neck, or expensive painting supplies were necessary to prop up the supplies in class, I would dig in my heels and utilise my voice to emphasise how ordinary I was. That conversation I'd picked up from the kids on my estate—which was never my own—turned out to be useful. I couldn't pretend to be like the other girls, so I became someone who was purposely unique and rough around the edges. When confronted with a uniform violation—the incorrect skirt, the wrong shoes—I discovered that if I raised my voice and shouted, "We can't afford the proper ones," or better yet, "I bought it in a charity shop," the teachers would back off. I found my power in the anxiousness that comes with claiming that you have less than others. If grammar school was supposed to make me a nice young girl, it turned me into an urchin. My speech changed again at university, now in the clipped tones of the truly aristocratic. I spoke more gently, making an attempt to pronounce my consonants correctly. When I came home for the holidays, I was told that university had transformed me, and that I had gone ahead of myself. So forth, so forth. My voice has turned into a chameleon that changes depending on who I'm conversing with. I don't even notice I'm doing it anymore, except when I have to communicate with people from two separate parts of my life at the same time. Then, unable to copy either, I'm obliged to follow the middle path, which is dreadful. Women's voices are challenged in ways that men's voices are not. We are considered as delicate mice if we speak too quietly, and strident if we raise our voices to be heard. Margaret Thatcher reportedly took elocution training early in her political career to project more authority. Gordon Reece, a senior television producer, was her mentor, and he guided her to a lower, more definite voice, dropping the plumminess in favour of something more regular and difficult to classify. Thatcher worked with a National Theatre coach to improve her breathing and verbal control, and she was not allowed to act angry or violent. Instead, she had to take on the personal tones of a mother or nanny, gently guiding us with firm assurance toward her decisions, or a lover, whispering her authority across a pillow.

Her voice had to bear the weight of the nation's suspicion of women while convincing them that we could think logically. It was forbidden to explicitly oppose the patriarchal; instead, it had to use words to coerce and lure it into obedience, all the while telling it that women were housewives and mothers, and Thatcher was just an anomaly of that natural feminine proclivity. Not a threat, but an effective tool for gaining a group of voters who were politically significant but culturally unimportant: women. Despite never having run for government, I had softened my voice in the same manner Thatcher did, learning to disturb its natural stridency and tone. People used to complain that I talked at them rather than to them, so I learned to add moments of false uncertainty to my sentences, such as ums and ers, to make myself appear more confused than I was. With the rain pounding on the glass, I allowed my voice to restore its fluency, immersing myself in the pleasure of my own speaking, the way my throat could fill with the resonance of my voice. I remapped it into four classes: lower, louder, softer, and slower. I'd learned to almost sing my words, blending them together like a river of notes or songbirds. My middle C returned, but it did not appear to be the most significant rise. My crackling had disappeared. My voice appeared smooth and silky when I talked now, as if it had been oiled. There was no more tickling or breaking. The words returned to me like silk. However, I was also relieved to be able to sing again. This particular winter, which saw the loss of my voice, had been a greater loss than I had realised. It wasn't about the pride of being able to trill a beautiful melody; it was about the delight of singing for the sake of singing. In 21st-century Britain, we have incorrectly equated singing with skill, which is fundamentally inaccurate. The right to sing is absolute, regardless of how it is seen by the rest of the world. We sing because we need to. We sing because it brings oxygen into our lungs and causes our hearts to soar with the notes we sing. We sing because it allows us to convey our emotions of love and sadness, happiness and desire, all encoded in lyrics that allow us to believe those sentiments are not totally our own. We have permission to express all of our heartbreaks and lusts via song. We may calm our children with songs while they are still too young to criticise our rusty voices, and we can find shortcuts to happiness while taking a daily shower or cleaning up the kitchen after yet another dinner. The finest aspect is that we can sing together, with entire families knowing the same songs and getting the same message. Every time I sing with my mother, I am shocked at how similar our voices sound. Hitting the same note in the exact same way results in a deep, genetic resonance. When I sing with my partner, our voices clash, but we sing songs that are meaningful to us, most often the wistful tones of "Wichita Lineman." When I sing with my son, I teach him more than just the words and melodies; I teach him how to survive. We, like the robin, sing to show our strength, but we also sing in anticipation of better days. We sing in either case.

CHAPTER 15

END

Every morning, I see a buzzard perched atop a fence near Manston Airport. He is big and grey, with his breast feathers in continual disorder. I like to think he's lived a little, and that he proudly displays his combat wounds. He is the only sentry this morning. As I fly by, I just see the yellow of his beak. I am beginning to suspect he is waiting for me here. He is my totem, my anchor for the day. He quiets the boiling tempest in my gut. He seems to be watching me.

I want this to end like a neat narrative arc should: life is settled and certain again; all of my issues and anxieties are addressed. I hope Bert is joyfully enrolled in a new school that is a wonderful fit for him, or that we have decided to abandon the concept of education entirely and gloriously, courageously venture out into the world on our own. I'd like to clarify that we have no plans to sell our property and relocate to a smaller, more affordable neighbourhood. I'd want to claim that I'm still not joking when I say that we should definitely move into that caravan in the woods because that's all we could afford on a regular basis. Instead, I am frequently tense with stress and sometimes feel as if we are only one step away from chaos. But I have to retain my calm for fear of transmitting my ongoing sense of separation from the world. I'm not feeling up to the job. For the thousandth time this year, I question whether I'm good enough.

To clear my mind, I take a walk around Pegwell Bay. Winter is coming to a close. We awoke a week ago to cold surrounding fields and white outlines around every leaf. Today is one of those enormous spring days, with huge blue skies dotted with clouds and playful gusts of wind that feel almost warm. Along the path, there are clumps of snowdrops and catkins that hang lime green from the hazel. The marshes were frozen solid just a few days ago, but they are now flowing, lapping, and rippling, waded by little egrets and sifted by curlews. I've heard that seals can be seen lounging at the creek's mouth. My fortune isn't on my side today. I promise myself that the next time I visit, I'll bring my binoculars.

As I walk, I remember Alan Watts' quote: "To hold your breath is to lose your breath." Watts offers an argument in The Wisdom of Insecurity that always persuades me but that I always forget: life is, by definition, uncontrollable. That we should renounce our efforts to finalise our comfort and security in favour of a profound acceptance of the unending, unpredictable change that is inherent in our existence. He says that human suffering is caused by our refusal to accept this fundamental truth: "Running away from fear is fear, fighting pain is pain, and trying to be brave is being scared." When you are in pain, your mind is in misery. The thinker's sole form is his thought. There's no way out.

Watts argues that we can only rely on the present moment: what we know and experience right now. The past has left us by. The future, on which we place so much emphasis, is an unstable element, utterly unknown, "a will-o'-the-wisp that ever eludes our grasp." When we focus over distant times, we miss out on amazing things happening right now. In reality, these unique things are all we have: the present now. Our senses' instant perception. When I return to Watts' art, a small, rebellious voice inside me cries, "That's not fair!" Some people lead a better life than others! However, this does not make his advice any less legitimate. Watts does not offer us a cheap, inflated solution to life's ups and downs. He isn't saying that if we can master this simple mental trick, all of our dreams will come true. He is telling the truth. Changes will continue to occur. The only thing we can control is our reaction.

Some concepts are too large to comprehend all at once. Here's one of them for me. Believing in the unpredictable nature of my life on this planet—accepting it passionately and deeply—is something I can only accomplish in fits and spurts. It is a practice in self-awareness. I remind myself of its potency, yet my conviction rapidly evaporates.

It reminds me once more. It floats away on the tide. This has no bearing on the power of the subsequent realisation or the next. I am willing to do it repeatedly throughout my life. I am willing to accept that it may never stick.

I see a movement in the air and turn to see a flock of birds rolling together at the sea's edge. I believed these were a swarm of starlings, but even at this distance, they're far too large. Rooks? A rookery less than a mile away has a swarm of undulating figures ascending from a couple of trees. It's a breathtaking sight, but not the same.

They are getting there. My arms have dropped to my sides, and I'm standing there, staring up at them. There is no greater thrill than this. This moment has grabbed every aspect of me: their incredible fluidity, the unspoken decisions that govern their movements. For a brief while, the group loses cohesiveness and scatters, leaving black polka dots over the sky. They appear to have been splashed with water. One flies overhead, followed by another with a white body and black wings rounded at the tips. Lapwing. I have never seen so many in my life. I had no idea they could do this.

I've recently noticed an increase in Facebook posts offering unsolicited advice on how to deal with a crisis: They say, for no apparent reason, "Hold on in there!" You have more power than you know. They're styled to resemble greeting cards, with pastel writing on dreamy backgrounds and words penned in exquisite cursive as if by a particularly inspiring friend. When I read them, I usually believe they're intended for a specific individual, that the person who posted them has noticed some sign of struggle and is sending an oblique word of support. Either that, or they are a cry for help, signals sent into the ether and returned to their senders.

This is where we are right now, constantly cheerleading ourselves into happiness while hiding the unpleasant underbelly of true reality. Those statements have always struck me as brutal: they offer next to nothing. There are days when I am certain that I am not strong enough to manage situations. And what happens if I can't keep going? So, what happens now? These people could as well be leaning into my face and saying Cope! Cope! Cope! while spraying perfume into the air to make everything look better. The underlying message in these texts is clear: unhappiness is not an option. For the sake of the audience, we must retain a positive attitude. While we no longer regard despair to be a failure, we anticipate that you will rapidly transform it into something valuable. And if you can't do that, attempt to disappear for a while. You are spoiling the atmosphere.

This is the inverse of caring. I've never believed, as some do, that social media is totally made up of manufactured lives and friendships, but I do think it's another place to exercise caution. The internet fosters a collector's mindset, with our social worth reduced to a single number. We must take care not to be duped by it. We must continue to examine the nature of those connections, their special meanings for us, and the nurturing that they may bring. Many of these friends, as in the real world, will disappear at the first sign of trouble. The only difference is that our missed connections are more visible online.

I'm beginning to believe that unhappiness is one of life's core pleasures: a raw, basic emotion that should be acknowledged, if not savoured. I would never advise for us to wallow in misery or avoid doing everything possible to alleviate it, but I do think it is instructive. After all, misery serves a purpose: it warns us when something is wrong. If we do not allow ourselves to be honest about our own sorrow, we will miss an important clue to change. We appear to be living in a period where we are bombarded with requests to be happy, while we are experiencing an avalanche of depression. We are told not to worry about small stuff, but we are always concerned. I often wonder if these are simply normal feelings that become terrible when denied. Much of life will undoubtedly be unpleasant. There will be moments when we can't wait to get out of bed, and times when we can't. Both are very normal. Both, in fact, require some perspective.

Sometimes the most straightforward response to our cries is the best one. We need someone who will cry with us, tolerate our misery, and allow us to be weak as we get back on our feet. We need people who understand that we cannot always cling on. That everything breaks every now and again. Short of that, we must perform those functions for ourselves: taking breaks when necessary and being kind to ourselves. We must discover our own grit throughout time.

When I started to write this book, I planned to travel the world in search of winter, visiting regions that were completely unfamiliar to me and interviewing people who I believed had wintered in extraordinary ways. I expected to discover more wisdom there than in my own backyard. I also reasoned that I could take a minute to write about wintering when I was in between winters, using the energy of the good periods to unravel the bad.

But along the road, life happened. Several winters arrived at once, as if I had unwittingly called them. My entire universe has shrunk, both practically and metaphorically. I wasn't able to do as much as I had planned. I couldn't be the cheerful, lively, and summery person I had imagined. I was struggling. Periods of hopelessness drew me down. Anxiety gnawed at me. There were times when I felt I couldn't write this, that I wasn't up to it, that doing so would result in some sort of embarrassing calamity simply for having the arrogance to think I had anything to say about the subject. Previously, this would have entirely consumed me for a season, and I would have emerged a year or two later, shaking my head and beginning again.

But I am here, and this is it. The only difference, and the reason I completed this, is experience. Winter felt familiar to me. I saw it coming (from a mile away, in case you're curious), and I looked it in the eyes. I embraced and let it in. I had several tricks up my sleeve. I had to learn them the hard way. When the heaviness of winter set in, I began to treat myself with the delicacy and devotion of a favoured kid. I assumed my wants were sensible and my feelings were an indication of something important. I ensured that I was properly fed and receiving enough sleep. I went for walks in the fresh air and spent time doing activities I like. I pondered what this winter was all about. I asked myself, "What is going to change?"

Nature shows that survival is a practice. Sometimes it thrives—lays on fat, garlands itself in leaves, and makes large amounts of honey—but other times it sacrifices itself to the essential needs of existence in order to survive. It doesn't do it once, resentfully, believing that one day it'll get it right and everything will be fine. Winter comes and goes in cycles, forever. Every day, it works on this. Winter is an essential part of the job for plants and animals. People are no exception.

To increase our winter survival abilities, we must first address our perception of time. We often think of our lives as linear, yet they are actually cyclical. Of course, I do not deny that we age, but we also have phases of good and bad health, optimism and deep anxiety, freedom and limitation. Everything looks to be simple at times and impossible at others. To make things easier, remember that our present will eventually become the past, and our future will become our present. That's because it has happened before. Things we put behind us frequently return to haunt us. Things that disturb us now will become history one day. Every time we go through the cycle, we increase the intensity. We learn from our failures and do a few things better the next time; we devise mental strategies to help us get through. This is how we progress. However, one thing is certain: we will have new issues. We'll have to grit our teeth and continue to survive.

Meanwhile, all we can do is cope with what is immediately in front of us. We perform the next necessary action, and then the next. That next action will appear delightful at some point along the path.

A year after leaving my job, I finally sorted through all of the literature that I had brought home from work. They had first acted as a sombre reminder of the person I was no longer, a fleeting image of myself that I had failed to realise. After a while, I forgot they were there, and they blended in with the rest of the clutter in my study.

They had lost some of their effectiveness by the time I got around to looking at them properly. At the time, I'd constructed my abscission zone, a gradual barrier between leaf and tree that permits dead matter to slide away effortlessly. My previous persona had died, unrequitedly. The guilt had disappeared. In retrospect, I had walked away from something that was potentially dangerous to me. I read each book in turn, sometimes with nostalgia and sometimes with disgust. Many of them made me wonder: were they really mine? What could I've done with them? I was pleased to put a number of them in carrier bags and take them to the local charity shop.

ACKNOWLEDGMENTS

I hope I remember to thank everyone who worked on this book.

First and foremost, I'd like to thank my interviewers for their generosity in time and willingness to explore difficult themes. Any errors are mine and not theirs. Richard Ashcroft also offered emergency philosophical consultation services.

Many thanks to Geoff Kloske, Kate Stark, Alison Fairbrother, Ashley Sutton, Helen Yentus, Lauren Peters-Collaer, Meighan Cavanaugh, Shailyn Tavella, and Ariana Abad from Riverhead. Most importantly, I'd like to thank Jynne Dilling Martin, who drew a far better book out of me through incisive and generous editing and a steady supply of cat photos. It's been a tremendous pleasure.

Thank you to Anna Hogarty, Hayley Steed, Madeleine Milburn, and the Madeleine Milburn Literary, Television, and Film Agency. It's tough to express how grateful and amazed I am that one of my book ideas has been taken seriously and treated with such care.

Finally, I'd like to thank Bertie for always pushing me to go further into this life. It's always worthwhile.

> *"We have seasons when we flourish and seasons when the leaves fall from us, revealing our bare bones. Given time, they grow again."*

Katherine May

The contents of this book may not be copied, reproduced or transmitted without the express written permission of the author or publisher. Under no circumstances will the publisher or author be responsible or liable for any damages, compensation or monetary loss arising from the information contained in this book, whether directly or indirectly. .

Disclaimer Notice:

Although the author and publisher have made every effort to ensure the accuracy and completeness of the content, they do not, however, make any representations or warranties as to the accuracy, completeness, or reliability of the content. , suitability or availability of the information, products, services or related graphics contained in the book for any purpose. Readers are solely responsible for their use of the information contained in this book

Every effort has been made to make this book possible. If any omission or error has occurred unintentionally, the author and publisher will be happy to acknowledge it in upcoming versions.

Copyright © 2023

All rights reserved.

Made in the USA
Columbia, SC
06 January 2025